초등학생의 영어 친구

리딩버디
READING BUDDY

2

리딩버디 2

지은이	NE능률 영어교육연구소
연구원	한정은, 강혜진, 이지연, 이윤주, 김은정
영문 교열	Lewis Hugh Hosie, Peter Morton, MyAn Le
디자인	장현정, 김연주
내지 일러스트	조희진, 양종은, 김동훈, 강난주, 진민지, 류미선, 강윤주, 최영아
내지 사진	www.shutterstock.com, www.flickr.com, www.commons.wikimedia.org
맥편집	이정임
영업	한기영, 이경구, 박인규, 정철교, 하진수, 김남준, 이우현
마케팅	박혜선, 남경진, 이지원, 김여진

Let's grow together

NE능률이
미래를
창조합니다.

건강한 배움의 고객가치를 제공하겠다는 꿈을 실현하기 위해
42년 동안 열심히 달려왔습니다.

앞으로도 끊임없는 연구와 노력을 통해
당연한 것을 멈추지 않고

고객, 기업, 직원 모두가 함께 성장하는 NE능률이 되겠습니다.

Dear Friends,

I'm your English Buddy!
Forget about all your worries.
I'm here to help you!
Let's smile! Let's learn! And let's have fun!

All the best,
Your English Buddy

★ HOW TO USE ★

재미있는 만화를 통해, 본문에서 배우게 될 내용과 문법을 확인해 보세요!

STORY

과학, 문화, 역사 등 다양한 주제에 대한 재미있고 정보성 가득한 이야기들이 수록되어 있습니다. 앞에서 배운 단어와 문법이 어떻게 쓰였는지 확인하며 독해 실력과 배경지식을 쌓아보세요!

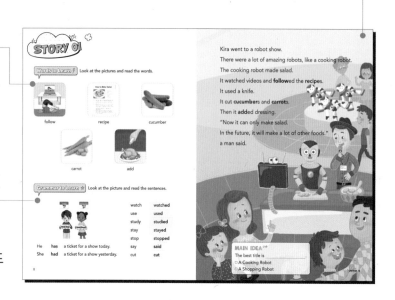

Words to Learn

본격적으로 이야기를 읽기 전에 이야기에 나올 단어를 사진이나 그림과 함께 미리 학습해 보세요!

Grammar to Learn

해당 Unit에서 배울 핵심 문법을 그림과 예시 문장으로 제시했습니다. 독해 실력에 기본이 되는 문법 실력을 한층 더 업그레이드 해 보세요!

Word Check

앞서 배운 단어를 문제를 통해 확인해 볼 차례입니다. 그림 및 사진과 맞는 단어를 찾아보며 단어 실력을 점검해 보세요!

Grammar Check

간단한 문법 문제를 통해 이야기에 등장한 주요 문법을 제대로 학습했는지 점검해 보세요!

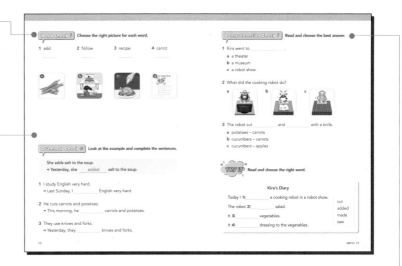

Comprehension Check

이야기를 잘 이해했는지 확인할 수 있는 문제들이 실려 있습니다. TRY IT 코너에서 조금 더 어려운 문제에도 도전하며 실력을 강화해 보세요!

재미있는 쉬어가기 코너를 통해 학습으로 지친 머리를 식혀보세요!

REVIEW TEST

각 Unit에서 학습한 단어와 문법, 그리고 이야기에 대한 이해도를 확인할 수 있는 다양한 문제가 실려 있습니다. 앞서 배운 내용을 다시 한번 확인해 보세요!

WORKBOOK

각 Unit에서 배운 단어와 문법을 여러 문제를 통해 확인하고 정리해 보세요.

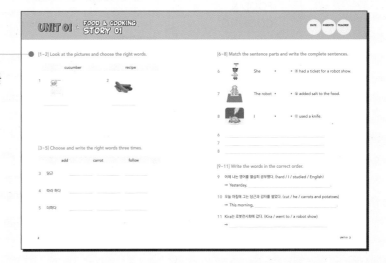

☆ OVERVIEW OF READING BUDDY ☆

	Unit	Title	Story	Key Words	Key Grammar
Level 1	01	INTERESTING PLACES	1	pilot, castle, wing, wall, museum	인칭대명사와 be동사
			2	vacation, hotel, have a meal, take a shower, feed, safe	명사의 복수형
	02	HEALTH	1	itchy, peanut, dangerous, see a doctor, take medicine	일반동사 현재형의 부정문
			2	gain weight, plate, taste, exercise, forget, hunger	명령문
	03	SPECIAL JOBS	1	perfect, lie down, leave, miss, chance	조동사 can
			2	pet, strange, worried, chew, swallow	be동사의 의문문
	04	HOBBIES	1	skate, jump, pass, fall down, hurt	일반동사의 3인칭 단수형
			2	collect, famous, touch, locked, unlock	want to-v
	05	NATURE	1	scared, hide, protect, bring, each other	형용사의 역할
			2	shine, sunny, sticky, get away, weak	조동사 can't
	06	SCHOOL LIFE	1	sweep, wipe, empty, trash can, erase, plant	It's time to-v
			2	get up, wash, get dressed, have breakfast, favorite	일반동사의 의문문
	07	SAVE THE EARTH	1	action, save the Earth, bottle, waste, recycle	청유문
			2	polar bear, the North Pole, spend, visit, tour, break	부정명령문
	08	FAIRY TALES	1	be lost, woods, cold, yummy, bread	There is/are
			2	magic, lamp, wish, comic book, cozy	Here is/are
Level 2	01	FOOD & COOKING	1	follow, recipe, cucumber, carrot, add	일반동사의 과거형
			2	astronaut, vegetable, hard, package, pour, microwave	의문사
	02	SPECIAL DAYS	1	the United States, celebrate, chocolate, interesting, each other	시간을 나타내는 전치사
			2	pick up, several, choose, athlete, rich	관사 the
	03	SUPERHEROES	1	prison, peace, delivery, fast, climb	조동사 will
			2	cape, resemble, attack, be afraid of, strong, train	등위접속사 and, but
	04	MY PET	1	apartment, bark, loudly, neighbor, allergic	셀 수 있는 명사와 셀 수 없는 명사
			2	grow, smart, smile, greet, guest	형용사의 순서

★ CONTENTS ★

STORY 01

follow

recipe

cucumber

carrot

add

Grammar to Learn ☆ Look at the picture and read the sentences.

| He | **has** | a ticket for a show today. |
| She | **had** | a ticket for a show yesterday. |

watch	watch**ed**
use	use**d**
study	stud**ied**
stay	stay**ed**
stop	stop**ped**
say	**said**
cut	**cut**

8

Kira went to a robot show.

There were a lot of amazing robots, like a cooking robot.

The cooking robot made salad.

It watched videos and **follow**ed the **recipe**s.

It used a knife.

It cut **cucumber**s and **carrot**s.

Then it **add**ed dressing.

"Now it can only make salad.

In the future, it will make a lot of other foods."

a man said.

MAIN IDEA ☆☆

The best title is _____.

☐ A Cooking Robot

☐ A Shopping Robot

Word Check ⚡ Choose the right picture for each word.

1 add   **2** follow   **3** recipe   **4** carrot

_____   _____   _____   _____

Grammar Check ☆ Look at the example and complete the sentences.

She adds salt to the soup.
➡ Yesterday, she ____added____ salt to the soup.

1 I study English very hard.
➡ Last Sunday, I _____ English very hard.

2 He cuts carrots and potatoes.
➡ This morning, he _____ carrots and potatoes.

3 They use knives and forks.
➡ Yesterday, they _____ knives and forks.

1 Kira went to _____.

   a a theater

   b a museum

   c a robot show

2 What did the cooking robot do?

  a    **b**    **c**

3 The robot cut _____ and _____ with a knife.

   a potatoes – carrots

   b cucumbers – carrots

   c cucumbers – apples

 **TRY IT** Read and choose the right word.

Kira's Diary

Today I **1)** _____ a cooking robot in a robot show.

The robot **2)** _____ salad.

It **3)** _____ vegetables.

It **4)** _____ dressing to the vegetables.

> cut
> added
> made
> saw

STORY 02

astronaut

vegetable

hard

package

pour

microwave

Grammar to Learn ☆ Look at the pictures and read the sentences.

What	does he eat?
Who	eats it?
When	does he eat it?

How	does she bake it?
Where	does she bake it?
Why	does she bake it?

12

What do **astronaut**s eat?

They eat food similar to ours.

They eat **vegetable**s, meat, and fruit.

They can even drink coffee.

But their food is dry and **hard**.

It is in a **package** with a tube.

How do astronauts cook their food?

It's simple and easy.

They just **pour** hot or cold water into the tube.

They heat it in a **microwave**.

MAIN IDEA ☆☆
The best title is _____.
☐ Space Food
☐ Astronauts' Health

Match the words to the pictures.

1 microwave   2 pour   3 astronaut   4 hard

Circle the correct word for each sentence.

1 Q: (What / Who) does he do on weekends?
   A: He does exercises.

2 Q: (Why / How) do you heat milk?
   A: I heat it in a microwave.

3 Q: (Where / When) did they meet Tim?
   A: They met him in Busan.

1 Astronauts eat food _____ to ours.

   a similar

   b strange

   c different

2 Astronauts' food is _____.

   a dry and hard

   b wet and soft

   c warm and sweet

3 How do astronauts cook their food? (Choose two.)

a    **b**    **c**

 Look at 'Today's Meal' and fill in the blanks.

Today's Meal

- meat with vegetables

  *Heat it in the microwave.

- coffee

Q: **1)** _____ do they eat?

A: They eat meat with vegetables.

Q: **2)** _____ do they cook it?

A: They heat it in the microwave.

Q: **3)** _____ do they drink?

A: They drink coffee.

REVIEW TEST

[1~5] Look at the pictures and write the right words.

| recipe | package | cucumber | follow | vegetable |

1 **2** **3** **4** **5**

[6~10] Choose and write the correct word.

6 I (added / followed) salt on the food. _____

7 (Packages / Astronauts) work in space. _____

8 She heats the food in a (microwave / pour). _____

9 They (pour / hard) milk into the cup. _____

10 The candy is too (hard / recipe). _____

11 Peter <u>watches</u> TV last night. _____

12 Q: <u>How</u> do you want to eat? _____

    A: I want to eat salad.

[13~14] Read and answer.

Kira went to a robot show.
There were a lot of amazing robots, like a cooking robot.
The cooking robot made _____.
It watched videos and followed the recipes.
It used a knife.
It cut cucumbers and carrots.
Then it added dressing.
"Now it can only make salad. In the
future, it will make a lot of other foods."
a man said.

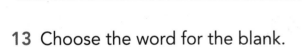

13 Choose the word for the blank.

    a soup

    b steak

    c salad

14 Check True or False.

    a In the show, there were many robots.   True   False

    b The cooking robot can make a lot of foods now.   True   False

    c The cooking robot followed the recipes in the videos.   True   False

멸종 위기의 판다를 구하는 싹다즌 방법

THE PANDA FONT PROJECT

⟨source: Ogilvy&Mather⟩

옆의 글씨체를 잘 살펴보세요! 무엇이 보이나요?
바로 판다입니다!
너무 귀여워서 미소 짓게 되는 이 글씨체는
누가, 왜 만들었을까요?
바로 세계자연보호기금(WWF)입니다!
이 단체는 세계의 멸종 위기 동식물 보호를 위해
애쓰는데, 이번에는 멸종 위기의 판다를
보호하고자 이 글씨체를 디자인했다고 하네요!
몇 개만 살펴볼까요?

엄마 판다가 새끼 판다를
업고 있네요!

'안녕~' 인사하는 판다!

새침한 뒷모습!

새끼 판다 두 마리가
뒹굴거리며 놀고 있네요!

'호잇!' 재롱부리는 판다!

STORY 01

the United States

celebrate

chocolate

interesting

each other

Grammar to Learn ☆ Look at the pictures and read the sentences.

February						
SUN	MON	TUE	WED	THU	FRI	SAT
1	2	3	4	5	6	7
8	9	10	11	12	13	14

March						
SUN	MON	TUE	WED	THU	FRI	SAT
1	2	3	4	5	6	7
8	9	10	11	12	13	14

He gets chocolates	**on**	Valentine's Day.
She gets candy	**on**	White Day.

Valentine's Day is	**in**	February.
White Day is	**in**	March.

Suji : Do you have White Day in **the United States**?

Nick : No, what is it?

Suji : It's like Valentine's Day.

But it's on March 14.

Nick : Cool! How do people **celebrate** it?

Suji : On White Day, only boys give girls candy.

In Korea, only girls give boys **chocolate**

on Valentine's Day.

Nick : **Interesting**! In the United States, boys

and girls give **each other** chocolate on

Valentine's Day.

Happy!! White Day!

MAIN IDEA ☆☆

The best title is _____.

☐ Boys and Girls

☐ White Day and Valentine's Day

Word Check ⚡ Match the words to the pictures.

1 each other **2** chocolate **3** interesting **4** celebrate

Grammar Check ☆ Circle the correct word for each sentence.

1 Valentine's Day is (in / on) February 14.

2 Christmas is (in / on) December.

3 (In / On) White Day, boys give girls candy.

4 My birthday is (in / on) November.

5 We eat *tteokguk* (in / on) New Year's Day.

1 In the United States, they don't have _____.

    a White Day

    b New Year's Day

    c Valentine's Day

2 White Day is on _____.

    a February 14

    b March 14

    c April 14

3 On Valentine's Day in Korea, _____ give _____ chocolate.

    a boys – girls

    b girls – boys

    c boys and girls – each other

 **Look at the chart and fill in the blanks.**

Children's Day

Country	Date
Korea	May 5
the US	the first Sunday in June

Suji : We have Children's Day in Korea.

Nick: Cool! When is it?

Suji : It is 1)_____.

       Do you have Children's Day in the US?

Nick: Yes, but it is 2)_____.

Words to Learn ⚡ Look at the pictures and read the words.

pick up

several

choose

athlete

rich

Grammar to Learn ☆ Look at the picture and read the sentences.

He picked up **a mike**. **The** mike means a singer.

She picked up **a ball**. **The** ball means an athlete.

Korean babies have a special party on their first birthdays.

At the party, babies **pick up** their future.

There are **several** things on a table.

The baby only **choose**s one of them.

It could be a mike, a ball, or some money.

The mike means a singer.

The ball means an **athlete**.

The money means a **rich** person.

Koreans call this *Doljabi*.

MAIN IDEA

The story is about is _____.

□ *Doljabi*

□ a 100-day party

1 athlete	2 several	3 pick up	4 rich
_____	_____	_____	_____

Grammar Check ☆ Circle the correct word for each sentence.

1 There is a ball on the table.
   (A ball / The ball) is red.

2 I ate cookies this morning.
   (Cookies / The cookies) were delicious.

3 He met a girl yesterday.
   (Girl / The girl) was very beautiful.

4 Max bought a camera.
   (A camera / The camera) was expensive.

1 _____ Korean babies have *Doljabi*.

  a One-year-old

  b Two-year-old

  c Three-year-old

2 At *Doljabi*, babies pick up their _____.

  a luck

  b names

  c future

3 Babies can pick up _____ thing(s) at *Doljabi*.

  a one

  b two

  c several

 **TRY IT** Read and fill in the blanks.

Jaehee

Minho

Yura

Jaehee chose the mike. She will be a(n) **1)** _____.

Minho chose the ball. He will be a(n) **2)** _____.

Yura chose the money. She will be a(n) **3)** _____.

REVIEW TEST

[1~5] Look at the pictures and write the right words.

| several | rich | the United States | chocolate | interesting |

1

2

3

4

5

[6~10] Choose and write the correct words.

6 We (celebrate / interesting) White Day. _____

7 We make (athlete / each other) happy. _____

8 The boy wants to be a(n) (athlete / several). _____

9 The baby (rich / picked up) money. _____

10 The baby (chocolate / chooses) the pencil. _____

the	a	on	in

11 In China, people eat noodles _____ New Year's Day.

12 Mike has a computer. _____ computer is new.

Korean babies have a special party on their first birthdays.
At the party, babies pick up their future.
There are several things on a table.
The baby only chooses one of them.
It could be a mike, a ball, or some money.
_____ mike means a singer.
_____ ball means an athlete.
_____ money means a rich person.
Koreans call this *Doljabi*.

13 Choose one word for the blanks.

   a A

   b An

   c The

14 Check True or False.

   a Korean babies do *Doljabi* on their 100th day .   True   False

   b Babies pick up three things at *Doljabi*.   True   False

   c The mike means a rich person.   True   False

영어 수수께끼

다음 질문에 해당하는 영어 단어를 맞혀보세요.

Q1. 영어 단어 중 가장 긴 단어는?

Q2. 문을 열 수 없는 열쇠(key)는?

Q3. 사람이 살지 않는 도시(city)는?

Q4. 두 개의 손(hands)이 있지만 박수칠 수 없는 것은?

Q5. 음료수(soda) 중 마실 수 없는 것은?

Words to Learn ⚡ Look at the pictures and read the words.

prison

peace

delivery

fast

climb

Grammar to Learn ☆ Look at the picture and read the sentences.

I	am	a student.	I	**will be**	a doctor.
I	study	hard to be a doctor.	I	**will help**	sick people.

Superman : All the bad guys are in **prison**!

Everyone can live in **peace**.

We need to find new jobs!

Batman : Yes! What will you do?

Superman : I will be a **delivery** man.

I can carry packages **fast**.

Spider-Man: I will be a window cleaner.

I can **climb** high buildings easily.

Batman : I will be a taxi driver.

I can drive and use my cool car.

Think!
What jobs can other heroes have?

1. _____
2. _____
3. _____

MAIN IDEA ☆☆
The best title is _____.
☐ Heroes' New Jobs
☐ Heroes' New Friends

Word Check ⚡ Choose the right picture for each word.

1 peace   **2** climb   **3** prison   **4** fast

_____   _____   _____   _____

Grammar Check ☆ Look at the example and complete the sentences.

He has a job.
➡ _____He will have a job_____ next month.

1 They clean their room.

➡ _____ tomorrow.

2 She drives a car.

➡ _____ next year.

3 I go camping.

➡ _____ this weekend.

1 Everyone lives in _____ because bad guys are in _____ .

    a peace – prison

    b prison – prison

    c prison – peace

2 Superman will be a _____ .

    a taxi driver

    b delivery man

    c window cleaner

3 Batman can _____ .

    a drive his cool car

    b carry packages fast

    c climb high buildings easily

 **Match and fill in the blanks.**

Who	Will be	Why
1) Superman •	• ① a taxi driver •	• ⓐ He can climb high buildings.
2) Spider-Man •	• ② a delivery man •	• ⓑ He can carry packages fast.
3) Batman •	• ③ a window cleaner •	• ⓒ He can drive and use his car.

Words to Learn ⚡ Look at the pictures and read the words.

cape

resemble

attack

be afraid of

strong

train

Grammar to Learn ☆ Look at the pictures and read the sentences.

Superman is fast **and** strong.

Batman can't fly, **but** he has a car.

Batman wears a black mask and **cape**.

He **resemble**s a bat.

But he didn't like bats.

They **attack**ed him when he was young.

He **was afraid of** them.

He wanted to be **strong**.

He **train**ed his body and mind.

He has good fighting skills.

He is not afraid of bats anymore,

but bad guys are afraid of him.

MAIN IDEA ☆☆

The best title is _____.

☐ The Story of Batman

☐ Best Friend of Batman

Match the words to the pictures.

1 train   **2** cape   **3** resemble   **4** attack

Grammar Check ☆ Circle the correct word for each sentence.

1 Batman (and / but) Superman are heroes.

2 I like bats, (and / but) Joe doesn't like them.

3 She is wearing a green hat (and / but) coat.

4 Bruce is strong (and / but) brave.

5 The book was very difficult (and / but) interesting.

Comprehension Check ⚡ **Read and choose the best answer.**

1 Batman doesn't wear _____.

 a sunglasses

 b a black mask

 c a black cape

2 Check True or False.

 a Batman liked bats when he was young.   True   False

 b Batman trained himself to be strong.   True   False

 c Batman is still afraid of bats.   True   False

3 Batman has good fighting skills, so _____.

 a he is afraid of bats

 b he wants to be strong

 c bad guys are afraid of him

 **Read and fill in the blanks.**

Causes		Effects
Bats 1)_____ Batman when he was young.	➡	He 2)_____ bats.
Batman wanted to be 3)_____.	➡	He 4)_____ his mind and body. He is not afraid of bats anymore.

REVIEW TEST

[1~5] Look at the pictures and write the right words.

train	peace	fast	strong	cape

1

2

3

4

5

[6~10] Choose and write the correct words.

6   A snake (attacked / strong) him.   _____

7   I (am afraid of / young) big dogs.   _____

8   My hobby is to (climb / mind) mountains.   _____

9   I (peace / resemble) my grandfather.   _____

10   He stole a car, so he is in (delivery / prison).   _____

40

11 James ordered a steak _____ salad.

12 I like pizza, _____ I don't like olives on it.

[13~14] Read and answer.

Superman : All the bad guys are in prison!
            Everyone can live in peace.
            We need to find _____!
Batman   : Yes! What will you do?
Superman : I will be a delivery man.
            I can carry packages fast.
Spider-Man: I will be a window cleaner.
            I can climb high buildings easily.
Batman   : I will be a taxi driver.
            I can drive and use my cool car.

13 Choose the words for the blank.

  a new jobs

  b new friends

  c new bad guys

14 Check True or False.

  a Everyone lives in peace now.   True   False

  b Heroes will have the same jobs.   True   False

  c Batman will be a taxi driver.   True   False

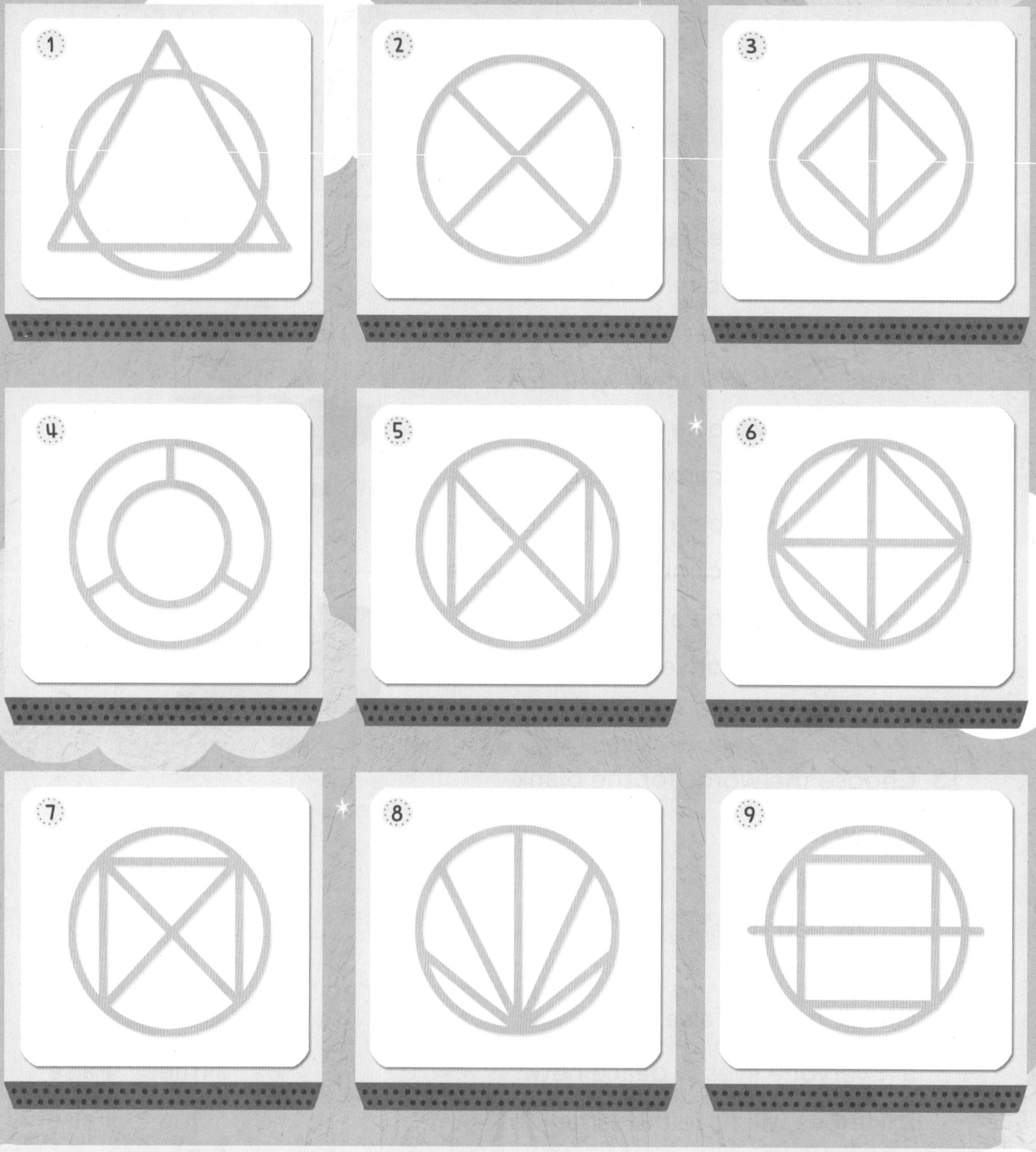

[정답] 한붓그리기가 가능한 도형은 1, 3, 5, 7, 9입니다.
홀수점(교차되는 선의 수가 홀수인 것)이 0개 또는 2개인 경우만 한붓그리기가 가능합니다.
홀수점이 0개이면 한붓그리기의 시작점과 끝점이 같고, 2개인 경우는 시작점과 끝점이 다릅니다.

다음의 도형들을 한 번에 그려보세요. 손을 떼지 않고 한 번에 그리기도 한붓그리기라고 해요?

둘째 한붓그리기

Words to Learn ⚡ Look at the pictures and read the words.

apartment

bark

loudly

neighbor

allergic

Grammar to Learn ☆ Look at the picture and read the sentences.

ø **Sara** is **an** elementary school student.

She has **a** dog. Its name is ø **Bob**.

It has ø brown **hair**.

Katie's family wanted a dog.

But it was difficult for them.

They live in an **apartment**.

It may **bark loudly**.

Their **neighbor**s may be angry.

And her mother is **allergic** to dog hair.

So, they got a robot dog, Fred.

It doesn't bark.

It doesn't have hair.

It is a lovely pet.

Her family is happy with it.

Think!
What are good things about having a robot dog?
1. _____
2. _____
3. _____

MAIN IDEA ☆☆
The best title is _____ .
☐ My Neighbors
☐ My Robot Dog

1 allergic **2** bark **3** neighbor **4** apartment

_____ _____ _____ _____

Grammar Check ☆ Circle the correct word for each sentence.

1 Susan is (ø / a) good student.

2 Charlie has (ø / a) red hair.

3 She is eating (a / an) apple.

4 My brother's name is (ø / a) Joe.

5 Tony's pet is (a / an) big snake.

Read and choose the best answer.

1 Katie can't have a dog because she _____.

   a hates pets

   b lives alone

   c lives in an apartment

2 Katie's mother is allergic to _____.

   a dust

   b cat hair

   c dog hair

3 Check True or False.

   a Fred is a robot dog.   True   False

   b Fred barks loudly.   True   False

   c Fred doesn't have hair.   True   False

 **TRY IT** Read and answer the question. (Choose two.)

Question: Who needs a robot pet?

Answer   : _____

Haley: My family likes dogs and cats, but my brothers are allergic to animal hair.

Alex : My family lives in a big single house. There is a big garden, too.

Luke : My family lives in an apartment. My neighbors hate noise.

STORY 02

grow

smart

smile

greet

guest

Grammar to Learn ☆ Look at the picture and read the sentences.

| It is a | **big happy** | pig! |
| People love this | **wonderful pink** | pig. |

Derek has a pet pig, Esther.

It was a small pink pig, but it **grew** so fast.

It is 300kg now!

He loves it very much.

It is **smart** and lovely.

It goes to the bathroom by itself.

It **smile**s and **greet**s **guest**s.

Some people don't understand him.

They say "Pigs are not pets!"

But this big clever pig is his family.

MAIN IDEA ☆☆

The best title is _____.

☐ A Lovely Pet Pig

☐ A Lovely Pet Dog

Word Check ⚡ Match the words to the pictures.

1 smart   **2** smile   **3** grow   **4** greet

 a

 b

 c

 d

Grammar Check ☆ Write the words in the correct order.

1 My teacher has _____(blond, long) hair.

2 She is wearing a _____(pink, pretty) shirt.

3 I want the _____(big, brown) teddy bear.

Comprehension Check ⚡ Read and choose the best answer.

1 Derek has a _____ as a pet.

  a cat

  b pig

  c dog

2 Check True or False.

a Esther is very small now.	True	False
b Esther is smart.	True	False
c Some people say "Pigs are not pets!"	True	False

3 What can Esther do? (Choose two.)

a    **b**    **c**

TRY IT Read and choose the right word.

This is my pet, Joy.

It is a **1)** _____ **2)** _____ rabbit.

It has **3)** _____ **4)** _____ ears.

I love my pet.

pink	small	white	long

REVIEW TEST

[1~5] Look at the pictures and write the right words.

apartment	bark	greet	smile	smart

1

2

3

4

5

[6~10] Choose and write the correct word.

6   Sue is (allergic / loudly) to dust.   _____

7   My dog is young. It is still (greeting / growing).   _____

8   My (apartments / neighbors) don't have pets.   _____

9   Many (guests / smiles) came to the party.   _____

10   Don't speak (smart / loudly) in the classroom.   _____

[11~12] Choose the right words.

11   grey short   short grey   a short grey

His cat has _____ hair.

12   white beautiful   a white beautiful   a beautiful white

I saw _____ whale in the aquarium.

[13~14] Read and answer.

Katie's family wanted a dog.
But it was difficult for them.
They live in an apartment.
It will bark loudly.
Their neighbors will be angry.
And her mother is allergic to dog hair.
So, they got a robot dog, Fred.
It doesn't bark.
It doesn't have hair.
It is a lovely pet.
Her family is happy with it.

13 Check True or False.

   a Katie's neighbors were angry because of her dog.   True   False
   b Katie's family doesn't have a pet now.   True   False

14 Katie got Fred because _____. (Choose two.)

   a it doesn't bark
   b it doesn't eat food
   c it doesn't have hair

동물들이 잠자는 모습

생김새와 사는 곳의 특수성 때문에 독특한 방식으로 잠자는 동물들이 있다고 하네요.
그들의 특별한 잠자는 모습을 살펴볼까요?

기린은 바닥에 주저앉은 채 긴 목을
구부려 바닥에 붙이고 잠을 잡니다.
상당히 불편해 보이는데요,
긴 목이 아프지는 않을지 걱정입니다.

해달은 물에 누워서 잔다고 합니다.
물에 떠내려가면 어쩌나 걱정되시나요?
다행히도 해달은 물살에 떠내려가지 않도록
다시마 같은 해조류를 자신의 몸에 감아
고정하거나 앞발로 꼭 쥔다고 하니
걱정하지 마세요!

황새는 한 다리로 서서 잠을 잡니다.
다리에 털이 없어서 다리를 들어 올려
몸에 꼭 붙여서 깃털로 감싼다고 합니다.
서 있던 다리가 아프면 다리를 바꾼 후
다시 잔다고 하네요.

STORY 01

Words to Learn ⚡ Look at the pictures and read the words.

first

sour

second

beak

third

Grammar to Learn ☆ Look at the picture and read the sentences.

People	call	me	Jim.
My mother	calls	me	a prince.
My friends	call	me	monkey.

There are three kinds of "kiwis" in New Zealand.

The **first** kiwi is a green, sweet and **sour** fruit.

The **second** kiwi is a bird.

It has a long **beak** and short wings.

It can't fly and it makes a sound like "kiwi."

People call it a kiwi.

The **third** kiwi means the people from New Zealand!

We call them Kiwis.

배경지식

키위새는 뉴질랜드에만 서식하는 새로, 뉴질랜드의 국가 새입니다. 뉴질랜드 원주민인 마오리족이 '키위키위'하고 우는 수컷의 재미 있는 울음소리를 듣고 '키위'라 부르기 시작했다고 합니다.

MAIN IDEA ☆☆

The best title is _____.

☐ Kiwis in New Zealand

☐ Fruits in New Zealand

1 third

2 sour

3 first

4 beak

_____

_____

_____

_____

Grammar Check ☆ Look at the example and complete the sentences.

The bird is a kiwi.
→ People ___call the bird a kiwi___.

1 The sour fruit is a lemon.
→ People _____.

2 David is a hero.
→ Everybody _____.

3 My sister is a genius.
→ My parents _____.

1 New Zealand has _____ kinds of kiwis.

  a two

  b three

  c four

2 The kiwi bird has a _____ beak and _____ wings.

  a long – long

  b long – short

  c short – long

3 The third kiwi means _____ from New Zealand.

  a flowers

  b clothes

  c people

 Read and choose the right word.

Kiwi

Q: Where does it live?

A: It lives in 1) _____.

Q: What sound does it make?

A: It sings 2) "_____."

Q: What can't it do?

A: It can't 3) _____.

| fly | kiwi | New Zealand |

STORY 02

invite

dessert

tooth

hold

coin

tradition

Grammar to Learn ☆ Look at the pictures and read the sentences.

It is a pretty doll.

What a pretty doll!

It was New Year's Day.

Dan's Greek friend, Irene, **invite**d him to dinner.

They ate Greek New Year's cake for **dessert**.

"Ouch! My **tooth**! What is this?" Dan said.

Irene laughed. Dan **held** a **coin** in his hand.

"Congratulations!

We put a coin into the cake. It means "luck."

You found it! What a lucky boy!"

What an interesting **tradition**!

MAIN IDEA ☆☆

The best title is _____.

☐ Delicious Food in Greece

☐ An Interesting Greek Tradition

Match the words to the pictures.

1 coin

2 invite

3 tooth

4 hold

Grammar Check ☆   Look at the example and complete the sentences.

He is a lucky boy.
→ What _____ a lucky boy _____ !

1 It is an interesting book.
   → What _____ !

2 They are cute puppies.
   → What _____ !

3 She is a smart girl.
   → What _____ !

1 On _____, Dan ate Greek cake with Irene.

   a Christmas

   b New Year's Day

   c Thanksgiving Day

2 According to tradition, Greek people put _____ into the cake.

   a candy

   b a coin

   c a ring

3 Who is the lucky person?

   a Dan

   b Irene

   c Irene's mom

TRY IT **Read and choose the right word.**

Irene 1)_____ Dan to dinner on New Year's Day.

⬇

They ate Greek 2)_____ for dessert.

⬇

Dan found a 3)_____ in the cake.

⬇

The coin means 4)_____ .

luck

coin

cake

invited

REVIEW TEST

[1~5] Look at the pictures and write the right words.

| second | tradition | sour | third | first |

1

2

3

4

5

[6~10] Choose and write the correct words.

6   David (invited / put) me to the party.   _____

7   Brian's (tooth / cake) hurt yesterday.   _____

8   Julie (called / held) green kiwis in her hand.   _____

9   Linda likes to collect (lucky / coins).   _____

10 The bird has a short (fruit / beak).   _____

[11~12] Write the words in the correct order.

11 (cake, what, delicious)

➡ _____ !

12 (exciting, trip, what, an)

➡ _____ !

[13~14] Read and answer.

It was New Year's Day.

Dan's Greek friend, Irene, invited him to dinner.

They ate Greek New Year's cake for dessert.

"Ouch! My tooth! What is this?" Dan said.

Irene laughed. Dan held a coin in his hand.

"Congratulations!

We put a coin into the cake.

It means "luck."

You found it! What a lucky boy!"

What an interesting _____ !

13 Check True or False.

a Irene invited Dan to lunch.   True   False

b Dan found a coin in the cake.   True   False

c The coin in the cake means "luck."   True   False

14 Choose the word for the blank.

a joke

b game

c tradition

세계에서 가장 무서운 놀이기구

1. Insanity - The Ride (인세니티)

미국 라스베이거스에 있는 이 문어발 놀이기구는 한 호텔 타워의
꼭대기에 있습니다. 높이가 약 340m인 이 호텔 타워는 미국
서부에서 가장 높습니다. 이 타워의 112층에 놀이기구가 있는
것이니 당연히 무서울 만하겠죠? 작은 의자의 안전벨트에 몸을
맡긴 채 무려 276m 상공에서 시속 64km로 빙글빙글 돈다고 합니다.

2. The Riddler's Revenge (리들러의 복수)

미국 로스앤젤레스의 한 테마파크에 있는 이 놀이기구는 세계에서
가장 높고 빠른 놀이기구입니다. 1,330m에 이르는 긴 트랙을
가졌으며 높이 48m에서 시속 105km로 달린다고 하네요. 또 깜짝
놀랄만한 점! 이 속도를 서서 견뎌야 한다고 합니다! 이 놀이기구를
타고나면 다리에 힘이 풀려서 다른 놀이기구는 타지 못할지도 몰라요.

3. Giant Canyon Swing (자이언트 캐니언 그네)

미국 콜로라도에 있는 이 놀이기구는 약 400m 높이의 절벽에
설치되어 있습니다. 이 놀이기구를 개발한 사람이자 놀이공원의
주인도 한 번 타보고 다시는 이 놀이기구를 타지 않을 정도로
아찔하고 스릴 넘친다고 합니다. 절벽에서 큰 그네를 타고 싶으신
분들 도전해 보세요!

STORY 01

symbol

around the world

wave

bill

wallet

Grammar to Learn ☆ Look at the pictures and read the sentences.

John Sam Mina

John is	from	the US.
Sam is	from	Ghana.
Mina is	from	Korea.

theater

| Jinho is | at | the theater. |
| | at | the front door. |

Ron wants to be the luckiest man in the world.

He collects **symbol**s of luck from **around the world**.

He put his cat doll at the front door.

It **wave**s its hand.

It is from Japan.

He carries a two-dollar **bill** in his **wallet**.

It is from the US.

Now, he wants a white elephant.

But he can't bring it from Thailand.

MAIN IDEA ☆☆
The main idea is _____.
☐ Ron collects symbols of luck
☐ Ron travels around the world

Word Check ⚡ **Match the words to the pictures.**

1 wave   **2** wallet   **3** symbol   **4** bill

Grammar Check ☆ **Circle the correct word for each sentence.**

1 This doll is (from / at) Mexico.

2 Emily is (from / at) the bus stop.

3 Brian and Patrick are (from / at) Canada.

4 Sora is (from / at) the French restaurant.

5 My mother is (from / at) the front door.

Read and choose the best answer.

1 Ron _____ because he wants to be the luckiest man in the world.

   a raises lucky animals

   b travels around the world

   c collects symbols of luck

2 Ron put his cat doll _____ .

   a on his desk

   b in his wallet

   c at the front door

3 Ron doesn't have _____ .

   a a cat doll

   b a two-dollar bill

   c a white elephant

TRY IT **Read and choose the right word.**

I have a symbol of luck.

It is a Matryoshka doll.

It is 1) _____ Russia.

I put it 2) _____ the front door.

It will bring me 3) _____ .

at   luck   from

Words to Learn ⚡ Look at the pictures and read the words.

mirror

broken

fence

sign

fail one's test

Grammar to Learn ☆ Look at the picture and read the sentences.

A dog is	**on**	the bed.
A hamster is	**in**	the box.
Two cats are	**under**	the chair.

72

Today I have a test.

This morning, I looked at the clock on the table.

It was 07:13.

The number 13! Bad luck!

I looked in the **mirror** on the wall.

It was **broken**!

More bad luck!

Now, I'm walking to school.

There is a black cat under a **fence**!

Three **sign**s of bad luck!

I will **fail my test**!

Think!
Do you know any other sign of bad luck?
1. _____
2. _____

MAIN IDEA ☆☆
The best title is _____.
☐ Three Signs of Bad Luck
☐ Three Signs of Good Luck

1 fence   **2** mirror   **3** sign   **4** broken

_____   _____   _____   _____

Grammar Check ☆ Look at the pictures and circle the correct word.

1 The clock is (on / under) the wall.

2 The mirror is (on / in) the box.

3 The black bird is (on / under) the fence.

1 The clock was _____ , and the black cat was _____ .

   a on the wall – on the table

   b on the table – under a fence

   c under the table – on a fence

2 When the girl looked in the mirror, it was _____ .

   a dirty

   b clean

   c broken

3 The girl saw three signs of bad luck, so _____ .

   a she will fail her test

   b she will break a mirror

   c she will see a black cat

 **TRY IT** Number the sentences in the correct order.

   1) _____   The girl saw a black cat.

   2) _____   The girl looked at the clock at 7:13.

   3) _____   The girl saw the broken mirror.

   4) _____   The girl was worried about her test.

REVIEW TEST

[1~5] Look at the pictures and write the right words.

| fence | mirror | sign | around the world | fail one's test |

1

2

3

4

5

[6~10] Choose and write the correct word.

6   I put the money in my (wallet / lucky).   _____

7   Sally has many (symbols / tests) of luck.   _____

8   I didn't have any (walls / bills) in my pocket.   _____

9   Dan washed the (broken / sign) plate.   _____

10 I (waved / carried) my hand to Tom.   _____

[11~12] **Fill in the blanks in each sentence.**

11 a   He is _____ the bed.

    b   He is _____ the US.

12 a   A key is _____ the chair.

    b   A wallet is _____ the chair.

[13~14] **Read and answer.**

Ron wants to be the _____ man in the world.
He collects symbols of luck from around the world.
He put his cat doll at the front door.
It waves its hand.
It is from Japan.
He carries a two-dollar bill in his wallet.
It is from the US.
Now, he wants a white elephant.
But he can't bring it from Thailand.

13 Choose the word for the blank.

    a richest

    b luckiest

    c happiest

14 Check True or False.

    a The cat doll from Japan waves its hand.   True   False

    b Ron has a two-dollar bill from Thailand.   True   False

    c Ron has a white elephant now.   True   False

기분에 따른 컬러 테라피

'컬러 테라피'란 속상하거나 혹은 마음의 안정을 찾고 싶을 때 색깔로
그 마음을 치유하는 것을 말합니다. 지금 여러분의 마음은 어떤가요?
마음 상태에 따라 다음의 색깔을 곁에 둬 보세요!

슬픔과 속상함을 느낄 때 (주황색)

주황색을 가까이해 보세요.
주황은 여러분이 어려움을 헤쳐나갈
수 있는 강인함을 줄 거에요!

힘이 없을 때 (빨간색)

빨간색을 가까이해 보세요.
빨강은 열정과 에너지를 불러
일으키는 효과가 있습니다.

나쁜 생각이 들고 숨고 싶을 때 (노란색)

노란색을 곁에 두세요. 노랑은 긍정적인
활력을 불어넣어 주는 색깔입니다!

급하고 여유가 없을 때 (파란색)

파란색을 가까이하세요.
파랑은 급한 여러분에게
마음의 여유를 줍니다.

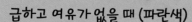

스트레스로 잠이 오지 않을 때 (보라색)

보라색을 곁에 두세요.
보라는 안정감을 주는 색깔이기
때문에 여러분이 편안하게 잘 수
있도록 도와줄 거에요.

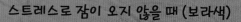

STORY 01

travel

careful

rule

subway

flush the toilet

pay a fine

Grammar to Learn ☆ Look at the pictures and read the sentences.

You **should** be careful.
follow the rules.

You **should not** eat anything.
drink anything.

80

I will **travel** to Singapore. I'm excited.

Wow! But you should be **careful**.

Why?

Some **rule**s there are different from Korea.

What are their rules?

You should not eat anything on the **subway**. And you should not feed birds in the park.

Anything else?

Flush the toilet after you use it, or you will have to **pay a fine**.

Thanks!

Singapore

MAIN IDEA ☆☆

The best title is _____ .

☐ Tips for Traveling Alone

☐ Some Rules in Singapore

1 subway   **2** travel   **3** rule   **4** careful

_____   _____   _____   _____

Grammar Check ☆ Look at the pictures and circle the correct word.

1 You (should eat / should not eat) in the library.

2 You (should be / should not be) quiet in the classroom.

3 You (should waste / should not waste) water.

1 Why does the boy go to Singapore?

   a to travel

   b to study

   c to visit his family

2 In Singapore, you should not _____ on the subway.

   a make a noise

   b eat anything

   c listen to the music

3 In Singapore, you should not _____ in the park.

   a eat snacks

   b feed birds

   c flush the toilet

TRY IT **Look at the signs and fill in the blanks.**

Other rules in Singapore!

You _____ should not smoke _____ on the subway. (smoke)

You 1)_____ in the zoo. (feed monkeys)

You 2)_____ on the street. (chew gum)

STORY 02

be made of

worry

sleeping bag

fun

afternoon

Grammar to Learn ☆ Look at the picture and read the sentences.

| She will | **go skiing**. |
| He will | **go camping**. |

Mom : Look, Tom!

Everything in this hotel **is made of** ice
— tables, chairs and beds!

Tom : Ice beds? Mom, we're going to be cold!

Mom : Don't **worry**.

We'll sleep in very warm **sleeping bag**s.

Tom : Oh, good! What are we going to do tomorrow?

Mom : After we have breakfast, we'll go ice skating!

Tom : Sounds like **fun**!

Mom : In the **afternoon**, we'll go ice fishing.

MAIN IDEA ☆☆

The best title is _____ .

☐ An Ice Bed

☐ An Ice Hotel

Match the words to the pictures.

1 worry   2 sleeping bag   3 fun   4 afternoon

Grammar Check ☆ Look at the example and complete the sentences.

> Peter wants to _____ go hiking _____ tomorrow. (hike)

1 Cindy will _____ next week. (swim)

2 Let's _____ in the afternoon. (shop)

3 I want to _____ this weekend. (ski)

Read and choose the best answer.

1 In this hotel, tables, chairs, and beds are made of _____.

 a ice

 b iron

 c wood

2 Tom and his mother will sleep in _____.

 a a tent

 b a warm room

 c sleeping bags

3 Tom and his mother will _____ tomorrow afternoon.

 a go shopping

 b go ice fishing

 c go ice skating

 **Number the sentences in the correct order.**

Tomorrow's Plan

 1) _____ They will go ice skating.

 2) _____ They will go ice fishing.

 3) _____ They will have breakfast.

REVIEW TEST

[1~5] Look at the pictures and write the right words.

| sleeping bag | be made of | subway | flush the toilet | afternoon |

1

2

3

4

5

[6~10] Choose and write the correct words.

6 We will have (fun / feed) tomorrow. _____

7 Joe will (travel / have) to Jejudo. _____

8 You should be (warm / careful) when you drive. _____

9 Don't (worry / sleep) about tomorrow's test. _____

10 Every country has different (rules / careful). _____

[11~12] Complete the sentences using 'should' or 'should not'.

11 You _____ stop at the red light.

12 You _____ eat anything in the museum.

[13~14] Read and answer.

I will travel to Singapore. I'm excited. 😆

Wow! But you should be careful.

Why? 😮

Some rules there are different from Korea.

What are their rules?

You should not eat anything on the subway.
And you should not feed birds in the park.

Anything else?

Flush the toilet after you use it,
or you will have to pay a fine.

Thanks! 😍

13 The boy is excited because _____.

   a he will feed birds
   b he will travel to Singapore
   c he knows the rules of Singapore

14 Check True or False.

   a The rules of Singapore are the same as Korea's.   True   False
   b People can eat food on the subway in Singapore.   True   False

세계 여행 컬러링

England

Australia

STORY 01

win

try one's best

terrible

wear

playground

step

Grammar to Learn ☆ Look at the picture and read the sentences.

last night

| He | watched | a movie last night. |
| She | **didn't watch** | a movie last night. |

Last week, Tim **won** the Smelliest Shoes Contest.

He **tried his best** to make his shoes smell **terrible**.

He **wore** them everywhere without socks

— inside the house, at the **playground**.

He **step**ped in dog-doo.

He also didn't wash his feet! Yuck!

He was happy to win.

But his friends didn't play with him anymore

because of his smelly shoes.

MAIN IDEA ☆☆

The main idea is _____.

☐ Tim won the Smelliest Shoes Contest

☐ Tim went to the playground without shoes

1 playground   2 wear   3 step   4 win

Grammar Check ☆ Look at the example and complete the sentences.

> Ellis won the contest last week.
> ➡ Ellis _____ didn't win _____ the contest last week.

1 You stepped on my foot yesterday.

➡ You _____ on my foot yesterday.

2 He washed his face this morning.

➡ He _____ his face this morning.

3 I tried my best in the test.

➡ I _____ my best in the test.

1 What did Tim do?

a  b  c

2 Tim was happy because _____ .

  a he had clean feet

  b he won the contest

  c he had many friends

3 Tim's friends _____ because of his smelly shoes.

  a didn't play with him

  b gave him new shoes

  c didn't wash their feet

 **Read and choose the right words.**

Q: Who was the winner of the Smelliest Shoes Contest?

A: Tim was the winner.

Q: What did the winner do to win the contest?

A: He **1)**_____ socks.

  He **2)**_____ in dog-doo.

  He **3)**_____ his feet.

didn't wear   didn't wash   stepped

STORY 02

Words to Learn ⚡ Look at the pictures and read the words.

stick

behavior

colorful

cover

start

Grammar to Learn ☆ Look at the pictures and read the sentences.

How long is the train?

How high is the train?

How many apples are there?

Come here! **Stick** your gum on the wall!

It is not bad **behavior**.

Colorful gum **cover**s the wall!

Q: Where is the wall?

A: It is in California.

Q: How long is the wall?

A: It is 20 meters long.

Q: How high is the wall?

A: It is 4.5 meters high.

Q: When did it **start**?

A: It started about 50 years ago.

MAIN IDEA ☆☆
The best title is _____.

□ Colorful Gum

□ Colorful Gum Wall

Word Check ⚡ Choose the right picture for each word.

1 start   **2** colorful   **3** stick   **4** behavior

___   ___   ___   ___

Grammar Check ☆ Circle the correct word for each sentence.

1 Q: (How many / How high) is this tree?
   A: It is 3 meters high.

2 Q: (How high / How long) is the ruler?
   A: It is 50 centimeters long.

3 Q: (How many / How long) books are in your bag?
   A: Three books are in my bag.

4 Q: (How long / How many) is the river?
   A: It is 481 kilometers long.

5 Q: (How long / How high) is the mountain?
   A: It is 8,848 meters high.

Comprehension Check ⚡ **Read and choose the best answer.**

1 People can _____ .

   a climb the wall

   b stick their gum on the wall

   c remove the gum on the wall

2 The gum wall is _____ long and _____ high.

   a 4.5 meters – 20 meters

   b 20 meters – 4.5 meters

   c 12 meters – 5.5 meters

3 Check True or False.

   a The wall is covered with colorful gum.   True   False

   b The wall is in California.   True   False

   c People started sticking gums about 40 years ago.   True   False

TRY IT Fill in the blanks.

Q: **1)** _____ is the Eiffel Tower?

A: It is in Paris.

Q: **2)** _____ is it?

A: It is 324 meters high.

Q: **3)** _____ was it built?

A: It was built about 120 years ago.

REVIEW TEST

[1~5] Look at the pictures and write the right words.

| step | try one's best | start | stick | cover |

1

2

3

4

5

[6~10] Choose and write the correct word.

6 (Colorful / High) flowers cover the table. _____

7 Telling lies is bad (contest / behavior). _____

8 The food smells (high / terrible)! _____

9 My favorite athlete (won / wore) the race. _____

10 John's dog likes to (win / wear) clothes. _____

[11~12] **Correct the underlined part in each sentence.**

11 He <u>didn't wore</u> socks yesterday. _____

12 Q: <u>How high</u> is the bridge? _____

A: It is 69.5 kilometers long.

[13~14] **Read and answer.**

Last week, Tim won the Smelliest Shoes Contest.

He tried his best to make his shoes smell _____.

He wore them everywhere without socks

— inside the house, at the playground.

He stepped in dog-doo.

He also didn't wash his feet! Yuck!

He was happy to win.

But his friends didn't play with him

anymore because of his smelly shoes.

13 Choose the word for the blank.

a good

b terrible

c different

14 Check True or False.

a Tim wore socks and went to the playground.   True   False

b Tim wasn't happy to win the contest.   True   False

c Tim's friends didn't like his smelly shoes.   True   False

나무를 그려봅시다

아래의 네모 상자 안에 나무를 마음대로 그려 보세요.

나무 개수

나무가 많을수록 믿을만한 친구가 많은 사람입니다.

나무 굵기

굵을수록 자기 자신에 대한 의식이 강합니다.

나뭇가지

가지가 굵을수록 집중력이 강하고, 얇게 그렸다면 변덕이 심합니다. 가지 수가 많으면 당신은 행동파이고, 적을수록 소극적인 편입니다.

나뭇잎

잎이 무성하다면, 호기심이 강하고 지적인 욕구가 강합니다. 미래에 대해서도 긍정적이네요! 적다면, 미래에 대해 비관적입니다.

열매

열매를 그린 사람은 성취감을 느끼는 상태입니다.

나무뿌리

뿌리를 튼튼하게 그렸다면 안정적인 상태이고, 약하게 그렸다면 불안감, 고민이 있는 상태입니다. 안 그렸다면 자신이나 현실에 대해 생각이 없는 상태입니다.

초등학생의 영어 친구

리딩버디

정답 및 해석

2

STORY 01 PP.8~11

Words to Learn

follow: 따라 하다　recipe: 조리법　cucumber: 오이
carrot: 당근　add: 더하다

Grammar to Learn

그는 오늘 전시회의 티켓이 있다.
그녀는 어제 전시회의 티켓이 있었다.

직독직해 P.9

Kira went / to a robot show.
Kira는 갔다 / 로봇 전시회에

There were / a lot of amazing robots, / like a cooking robot.
~이 있었다 / 많은 놀라운 로봇들이 / 요리하는 로봇과 같은

The cooking robot made / salad.
그 요리하는 로봇은 만들었다 / 샐러드를

It watched videos / and followed the recipes.
그것은 동영상을 보았다 / 그리고 조리법을 따라했다

It used / a knife.
그것은 사용했다 / 칼을

It cut / cucumbers and carrots.
그것은 썰었다 / 오이와 당근을

Then / it added / dressing.
그 다음에 / 그것은 더했다 / 드레싱을

"Now / it can / only make salad.
지금 / 그것은 ~할 수 있다 / 샐러드만을 만든다

In the future, / it will make / a lot of other foods." / a man said.
미래에 / 그것은 만들 것이다 / 많은 다른 음식을 / 한 남자가 말했다

본문해석

Kira는 로봇 전시회에 갔다.
요리하는 로봇과 같은 놀라운 로봇이 많이 있었다.
요리하는 로봇은 샐러드를 만들었다.
그것은 비디오를 보고 조리법을 따라 했다.
그것은 칼을 사용했다.
그것은 오이와 당근을 썰었다.
그 다음에 그것은 드레싱을 더했다.
"현재 그것은 샐러드밖에 만들 수 없습니다.

미래에 그것은 많은 다른 음식을 만들 것입니다."
한 남자가 말했다.

정답

MAIN IDEA

A Cooking Robot

Word Check

1 ⓒ　2 ⓑ　3 ⓓ　4 ⓐ

Grammar Check

1 studied　2 cut　3 used

1 지난 일요일에 나는 영어를 매우 열심히 공부했다.
2 오늘 아침에 그는 당근과 감자를 썰었다.
3 어제 그들은 칼과 포크를 사용했다.

Comprehension Check

1 c　2 a　3 b

1 Kira는 로봇 전시회에 갔다.
2 요리하는 로봇은 무엇을 했는가?
3 로봇은 칼로 오이와 당근을 썰었다.

TRY IT

1) saw　2) made　3) cut　4) added

Kira의 일기
오늘 나는 로봇 전시회에서 요리하는 로봇을 보았다.
로봇은 샐러드를 만들었다.
그것은 채소를 썰었다.
그것은 채소에 드레싱을 더했다.

STORY 02 PP.12~15

Words to Learn

astronaut: 우주비행사　vegetable: 채소　hard: 딱딱한
package: (포장용) 봉지　pour: 붓다
microwave: 전자레인지

Grammar to Learn

그는 무엇을 먹나요?
누가 그것을 먹나요?

그가 언제 그것을 먹나요?

그녀는 어떻게 그것을 굽나요?
그녀는 어디서 그것을 굽나요?
그녀는 왜 그것을 굽나요?

직독직해 P.13

What / do astronauts eat?
무엇을 / 우주비행사들은 먹는가

They eat / food similar / to ours.
그들은 먹는다 / 비슷한 음식을 / 우리의 것과

They eat / vegetables, meat, and fruit.
그들은 먹는다 / 채소, 고기 그리고 과일을

They can / even / drink coffee.
그들은 ~할 수 있다 / 심지어 / 커피를 마시다

But / their food is / dry and hard.
그러나 / 그들의 음식은 ~이다 / 건조하고 딱딱한

It is / in a package / with a tube.
그것은 있다 / 봉지 안에 / 튜브가 있는

How / do astronauts cook / their food?
어떻게 / 우주비행사들은 요리하는가 / 그들의 음식을?

It's / simple and easy.
그것은 ~이다 / 간단하고 쉬운

They just pour / hot or cold water / into the tube.
그들은 단지 붓는다 / 뜨겁거나 차가운 물을 / 튜브 안으로

They heat it / in a microwave.
그들은 그것을 데운다 / 전자레인지에서

본문해석

우주비행사들은 무엇을 먹을까요?
그들은 우리의 것과 비슷한 음식을 먹습니다.
그들은 채소와 고기, 과일을 먹습니다.
그들은 심지어 커피도 마실 수 있습니다.
그러나 그들의 음식은 건조하고 딱딱합니다.
그것은 튜브가 있는 포장용 봉지에 있습니다.
우주인들은 그들의 음식을 어떻게 요리할까요?
그것은 간단하고 쉽습니다.
그들은 그냥 뜨겁거나 차가운 물을 튜브 안으로 붓습니다.
그들은 그것을 전자레인지에서 데웁니다.

정답

MAIN IDEA

Space Food

Word Check

1 ⓑ   2 ⓐ   3 ⓓ   4 ⓒ

Grammar Check

1 What   2 How   3 Where

1 Q: 그는 주말에 무엇을 하나요?
　 A: 그는 운동을 합니다.
2 Q: 당신은 어떻게 우유를 데우나요?
　 A: 나는 전자레인지에 데웁니다.
3 Q: 그들은 어디에서 Tim을 만났나요?
　 A: 그들은 그를 부산에서 만났습니다.

Comprehension Check

1 a   2 a   3 b, c

1 우주비행사들은 우리의 것과 비슷한 음식을 먹는다.
2 우주비행사들의 음식은 건조하고 딱딱하다.
3 우주비행사들은 어떻게 그들의 음식을 요리하는가?

TRY IT

1) What   2) How   3) What

Q: 그들은 무엇을 먹나요?
A: 그들은 고기와 채소를 먹습니다.
Q: 그들은 그것을 어떻게 요리하나요?
A: 그들은 그것을 전자레인지에 데웁니다.
Q: 그들은 무엇을 마시나요?
A: 그들은 커피를 마십니다.

REVIEW TEST PP.15-17

1 cucumber   2 vegetable   3 package
4 recipe   5 follow   6 added   7 Astronauts
8 microwave   9 pour   10 hard   11 watched
12 What   13 c   14 a True   b False   c True

1　cucumber: 오이
2　vegetable: 채소
3　package: (포장용) 봉지
4　recipe: 조리법
5　follow: 따라 하다
6　나는 음식에 소금을 더했다.
7　우주비행사들은 우주에서 일한다.
8　그녀는 음식을 전자레인지에서 데운다.
9　그들은 우유를 컵에 붓는다.
10　이 사탕은 너무 딱딱하다.
11　Peter는 어젯밤에 TV를 보았다.
12　Q: 무엇을 먹고 싶나요?
　　A: 나는 샐러드가 먹고 싶어요.
14　a 전시회에는 많은 로봇이 있었다.
　　b 현재 요리하는 로봇은 많은 음식들을 만들 수 있다.
　　c 요리하는 로봇은 비디오의 조리법의 따라 했다.

UNIT 02 SPECIAL DAYS

STORY 01 PP.20~23

Words to Learn

the United States: 미국   celebrate: 기념하다
chocolate: 초콜릿   interesting: 흥미로운, 재미있는
each other: 서로

Grammar to Learn

그는 밸런타인데이에 초콜릿을 받는다.
그녀는 화이트데이에 사탕을 받는다.

밸런타인데이는 2월이다.
화이트데이는 3월이다.

직독직해 P.21

Suji : Do you have / White Day / in the United
States?
너희는 있니 / 화이트데이가 / 미국에는

Nick: No, / what / is it?
아니, / 무엇 / 그것은 ~이니?

Suji : It's / like Valentine's Day.
그것은 ~이다 / 밸런타인데이 같은
But it's / on March 14.
그러나 그것은 ~이다 / 3월 14일

Nick: Cool!
멋지다
How / do peopl celebrate it?
어떻게 / 사람들이 그것을 기념하니

Suji : On White Day, / only boys / give girls candy.
화이트데이에 / 남자들만이 / 여자들에게 사탕을 준다
In Korea, / only girls / give boys chocolate
/ on Valentine's Day.
한국에서 / 여자들만이 / 남자들에게 초콜릿을 준다 /
밸런타인데이에

Nick: Interesting! / In the United States, / boys
and girls / give each other / chocolate / on
Valentine's Day.
흥미롭다 / 미국에서는 / 남자들과 여자들이 / 서로에
게 준다 / 초콜릿을 / 밸런타인데이에

본문해석

Suji : 미국에는 화이트데이가 있니?
Nick: 아니, 그게 뭔데?
Suji : 밸런타인데이 같은 거야.
하지만 그것은 3월 14일이야.

Nick: 멋지다! 사람들이 그걸 어떻게 기념하는데?
Suji : 화이트데이에는 남자들만 여자들에게 사탕을 줘.
한국에서는 밸런타인데이에 여자들만 남자들에게
초콜릿을 주거든.
Nick: 흥미롭다! 미국에서는, 밸런타인데이에 남자와 여
자가 서로에게 초콜릿을 줘.

정답

MAIN IDEA

White Day and Valentine's Day

Word Check

1 ⓐ   2 ⓒ   3 ⓓ   4 ⓑ

Grammar Check

1 on   2 in   3 On   4 in   5 on

1 밸런타인데이는 2월 14일이다.
2 크리스마스는 12월이다.
3 화이트데이에 남자들은 여자들에게 사탕을 준다.
4 내 생일은 11월이다.
5 우리는 설날에 떡국을 먹는다.

Comprehension Check

1 a   2 b   3 b

1 미국에는 화이트데이가 없다.
2 화이트데이는 3월 14일이다.
3 한국에서는 밸런타인데이에 여자들이 남자들에게 초콜릿을
준다.

TRY IT

1) on May 5   2) on the first Sunday in June

Suji: 한국에는 어린이날이 있어.
Nick: 멋지다! 그게 언제야?
Suji: 5월 5일이야.
미국에도 어린이날이 있니?
Nick: 응, 하지만 그것은 6월의 첫 번째 일요일이야.

STORY 02 PP.24~27

Words to Learn

pick up: 집어 들다   several: 몇몇의   choose: 고르다

athlete: 운동 선수 rich: 부유한

Grammar to Learn

그는 마이크를 집어 들었다.
그 마이크는 가수를 의미한다.
그녀는 공을 집어 들었다.
그 공은 운동선수를 의미한다.

직독직해 `P.25`

Korean babies / have a special party / on their first birthdays.
한국의 아기들은 / 특별한 파티를 한다 / 그들의 첫 번째 생일에
At the party, / babies pick up / their future.
파티에서 / 아기들은 집어 든다 / 그들의 미래를
There are / several things / on a table.
~이 있다 / 몇 가지 물건들 / 상 위에
The baby only chooses / one of them.
아기는 ~만을 고른다 / 그 중 하나
It could be / a mike, a ball, / or some money.
그것은 ~일 수 있다 / 마이크, 공 / 혹은 돈
The mike means / a singer.
마이크는 의미한다 / 가수를
The ball means / an athlete.
공은 의미한다 / 운동 선수를
The money means / a rich person.
돈은 의미한다 / 부유한 사람을
Koreans / call this / *Doljabi*.
한국인들은 / 이것을 부른다 / '돌잡이'라고

본문해석

한국 아기들은 그들의 첫 번째 생일에 특별한 파티를 한다.
그 파티에서 아기들은 그들의 미래를 집어 든다.
상에는 몇 가지 물건들이 있다.
아기는 그 중에서 하나만 고른다.
그것은 마이크, 공, 혹은 돈이 될 수도 있다.
그 마이크는 가수를 의미한다.
그 공은 운동선수를 의미한다.
그 돈은 부자를 의미한다.
한국인들은 이것을 '돌잡이'라고 부른다.

정답

MAIN IDEA

Doljabi

Word Check

1 ⓑ 2 ⓓ 3 ⓒ 4 ⓐ

Grammar Check

1 The ball 2 The cookies 3 The girl
4 The camera

1 테이블 위에 공이 하나 있다. 그 공은 빨간색이다.
2 나는 오늘 아침에 쿠키를 먹었다. 그 쿠키들은 맛있었다.
3 그는 어제 한 소녀를 만났다. 그 소녀는 매우 아름다웠다.
4 Max는 사진기를 샀다. 그 사진기는 비쌌다.

Comprehension Check

1 a 2 c 3 a

1 한 살짜리 한국 아기들은 '돌잡이'를 한다.
2 '돌잡이'에서 아기들은 그들의 미래를 집어 든다.
3 아기들은 '돌잡이'에서 하나의 물건을 집을 수 있다.

TRY IT

1) singer 2) athlete 3) rich person

재희는 마이크를 골랐다. 그녀는 가수가 될 것이다.
민호는 공을 골랐다. 그는 운동선수가 될 것이다.
유라는 돈을 골랐다. 그녀는 부자가 될 것이다.

REVIEW TEST `PP. 28-29`

1 chocolate 2 rich 3 several 4 the United States 5 interesting 6 celebrate 7 each other 8 athlete 9 picked up 10 chooses 11 on 12 The 13 c 14 a False b False c False

1 chocolate: 초콜릿
2 rich: 부유한
3 several: 몇몇의
4 the United States: 미국
5 interesting: 흥미로운, 재미있는
6 우리는 화이트데이를 기념한다.
7 우리는 서로를 행복하게 한다.
8 소년은 운동선수가 되고 싶어한다.
9 그 아기는 돈을 집어 들었다.
10 그 아기는 연필을 고른다.
11 중국에서는 새해에 국수를 먹는다.
12 Mike는 컴퓨터를 가지고 있다. 그 컴퓨터는 새것이다.
14 a 한국 아기들은 100일에 '돌잡이'를 한다.
    b 아기들은 '돌잡이'에서 세 개의 물건을 집어 든다.
    c 마이크는 부자를 의미한다.

UNIT 03 SUPERHEROES

STORY 01 PP.32~35

Words to Learn

prison: 감옥   peace: 평화   delivery: 배달   fast: 빠르게
climb: 오르다

Grammar to Learn

나는 학생이다.
나는 의사가 되기 위해 열심히 공부한다.
나는 의사가 될 것이다.
나는 아픈 사람들을 도울 것이다.

직독직해 P.33

Superman : All the bad guys are / in prison!
　　　　　　모든 나쁜 사람들이 있다 / 감옥에
　　　　　　Everyone can live / in peace.
　　　　　　모두가 살 수 있다 / 평화롭게
　　　　　　We need to / find new jobs!
　　　　　　우리는 ~해야 한다 / 새로운 직업을 찾다
Batman : Yes! / What / will you do?
　　　　　　맞다 / 무엇을 / 넌 할거니
Superman : I will be / a delivery man.
　　　　　　나는 ~이 될 것이다 / 배달원
　　　　　　I can / carry packages / fast.
　　　　　　나는 ~할 수 있다 / 소포들을 나르다 / 빠르게
Spider-Man: I will be / a window cleaner.
　　　　　　나는 ~이 될 것이다 / 창문닦이
　　　　　　I can climb / high buildings / easily.
　　　　　　나는 올라갈 수 있다 / 높은 건물들을 / 쉽게
Batman : I will be / a taxi driver.
　　　　　　나는 ~이 될 것이다 / 택시 운전사
　　　　　　I can / drive / and use my cool car.
　　　　　　나는 ~할 수 있다 / 운전하고 / 내 멋진 자동
　　　　　　차를 이용하다

본문해석

슈퍼맨 : 모든 악당들은 감옥에 있어!
　　　　 모든 사람들이 평화롭게 살 수 있어.
　　　　 우리는 새로운 직업을 찾아야 해!
배트맨 : 맞아! 넌 무엇을 할 거니?
슈퍼맨 : 나는 배달원이 될 거야.
　　　　 나는 소포를 빠르게 나를 수 있어.
스파이더맨: 나는 창문닦이가 될 거야.
　　　　 나는 높은 빌딩을 쉽게 오를 수 있어.

배트맨 　 : 나는 택시 운전사가 될 거야.
　　　　　 나는 운전할 수 있고 내 멋진 자동차를 이용
　　　　　 할 수 있어.

정답

MAIN IDEA

Heroes' New Jobs

Word Check

1 ⓒ   2 ⓑ   3 ⓓ   4 ⓐ

Grammar Check

1 They will clean their room
2 She will drive a car
3 I will go camping

1 그들은 내일 그들의 방을 청소할 것이다.
2 그녀는 내년에 자동차를 운전할 것이다.
3 나는 이번 주말에 캠핑하러 갈 것이다.

Comprehension Check

1 a   2 b   3 a

1 모든 사람들이 평화롭게 사는데, 악당들이 감옥에 있기 때문이다.
2 슈퍼맨은 배달원이 될 것이다.
3 배트맨은 그의 멋진 자동차를 운전할 수 있다.

TRY IT

1) ② - ⓑ   2) ③ - ⓐ   3) ① - ⓒ

1 슈퍼맨 – 배달원 – 그는 소포를 빨리 나를 수 있다.
2 스파이더맨 – 창문닦이 – 그는 높은 건물을 오를 수 있다.
3 배트맨 – 택시 운전사 – 그는 운전할 수 있고 그의 자동차를 이용한다.

STORY 02 PP.36~39

Words to Learn

cape: 망토   resemble: 닮다   attack: 공격하다
be afraid of: 두려워하다   strong: 강한
train: 단련하다, 훈련하다

Grammar to Learn

슈퍼맨은 빠르고 강하다.

배트맨은 날 수 없지만, 자동차를 가지고 있다.

직독직해 P.39

Batman wears / a black mask and cape.

배트맨은 입는다 / 검은 마스크와 망토를

He resembles / a bat.

그는 닮았다 / 박쥐를

But / he didn't like / bats.

그러나 / 그는 좋아하지 않았다 / 박쥐를

They attacked / him / when he was young.

그것들은 공격했다 / 그를 / 그가 어렸을 때

He was afraid of / them.

그는 두려워했다 / 그것들을

He wanted / to be strong.

그는 원했다 / 강해지기를

He trained / his body and mind.

그는 단련했다 / 그의 몸과 마음을

He has / good fighting skills.

그는 지녔다 / 훌륭한 전투 기술을

He is not afraid of bats / anymore, / but bad guys / are afraid of him.

그는 박쥐를 두려워하지 않는다 / 더 이상 / 그러나 나쁜 사람들은 / 그를 두려워한다

본문해석

배트맨은 검은 마스크와 망토를 걸친다.

그는 박쥐를 닮았다.

그러나 그는 박쥐를 좋아하지 않았다.

그가 어렸을 때 그것들이 그를 공격했다.

그는 그것들을 두려워했다.

그는 강해지고 싶었다.

그는 그의 몸과 마음을 단련했다.

그는 훌륭한 전투 기술을 지니고 있다.

그는 더 이상 박쥐를 두려워하지 않지만, 악당들은 그를 두려워한다.

정답

MAIN IDEA

The Story of Batman

Word Check

1 ⓓ   2 ⓐ   3 ⓑ   4 ⓒ

Grammar Check

1 and   2 but   3 and   4 and   5 but

1 배트맨과 슈퍼맨은 히어로들이다.

2 나는 박쥐를 좋아하지만, Joe는 그것들을 좋아하지 않는다.

3 그녀는 녹색 모자와 코트를 입고 있다.

4 Bruce는 강하고 용감하다.

5 그 책은 매우 어렵지만 흥미로웠다.

Comprehension Check

1 a   2 a False b True c False   3 c

1 배트맨은 선글라스를 쓰지 않는다.

2 a 배트맨은 어렸을 때 박쥐를 좋아했다.

  b 배트맨은 강해지기 위해 자신을 단련했다.

  c 배트맨은 아직도 박쥐를 두려워한다.

3 배트맨은 훌륭한 전투 기술을 지녀서, 악당들이 그를 두려워한다.

TRY IT

1) attacked   2) was afraid of   3) strong

4) trained

배트맨이 어렸을 때 박쥐들이 그를 공격했다.

그는 박쥐를 두려워했다.

배트맨은 강해지고 싶었다.

그는 그의 마음과 몸을 단련했다.

그는 더 이상 박쥐를 두려워하지 않는다.

REVIEW TEST PP. 40~41

1 fast   2 strong   3 cape   4 train   5 peace
6 attacked   7 am afraid of   8 climb
9 resemble   10 prison   11 and   12 but
13 a   14 a True b False c True

1   fast: 빠르게   2   strong: 강한

3   cape: 망토   4   train: 단련하다, 훈련하다

5   peace: 평화

6   뱀이 그를 공격했다.   7   나는 큰 개들을 두려워한다.

8   내 취미는 산을 오르는 것이다.

9   나는 우리 할아버지를 닮았다.

10 그는 자동차를 훔쳐서, 감옥에 있다.

11 James는 스테이크와 샐러드를 주문했다.

12 나는 피자를 좋아하지만, 그것 위의 올리브는 좋아하지 않는다.

14 a 이제 모든 사람이 평화롭게 지낸다.

    b 히어로들은 같은 직업을 가질 것이다.

    c 배트맨은 택시 운전사가 될 것이다.

STORY 01 PP.44~47

Words to Learn

apartment: 아파트 bark: 짖다 loudly: 큰 소리로
neighbor: 이웃(사람) allergic: 알레르기가 있는

Grammar to Learn

Sara는 초등학생이다.
그녀는 개 한 마리를 가지고 있다. 그것의 이름은 Bob이다.
그것은 갈색 털을 가지고 있다.

직독직해 P.45

Katie's family wanted / a dog.
Katie의 가족은 원했다 / 개를
But / it was difficult / for them.
그러나 / 그것은 어려웠다 / 그들에게
They live / in an apartment.
그들은 산다 / 아파트 안에
It may bark / loudly.
그것은 짖을지도 모른다 / 큰 소리로
Their neighbors / may be angry.
그들의 이웃들은 / 화낼지도 모른다
And her mother / is allergic / to dog hair.
그리고 그녀의 엄마는 / 알레르기가 있다 / 개털에
So, they got / a robot dog, Fred.
그래서 그들은 얻었다 / 로봇개 Fred를
It doesn't bark.
그것은 짖지 않는다
It doesn't have / hair.
그것은 가지고 있지 않다 / 털을
It is / a lovely pet.
그것은 ~이다 / 사랑스러운 애완동물
Her family is happy / with it.
그녀의 가족은 행복하다 / 그것과 함께

본문해석

Katie의 가족은 개를 원했다.
그러나 그것은 그들에게 어려웠다.
그들은 아파트에 산다.
그것은 큰 소리로 짖을지도 모른다.
그들의 이웃들은 화낼지도 모른다.
그리고 그녀의 엄마는 개털에 알레르기가 있다.
그래서 그들은 로봇개 Fred를 데려왔다.

그것은 짖지 않는다.
그것은 털이 없다.
그것은 사랑스러운 애완동물이다.
그녀의 가족은 그것과 함께여서 행복하다.

정답

MAIN IDEA

My Robot Dog

Word Check

1 ⓑ 2 ⓒ 3 ⓐ 4 ⓓ

Grammar Check

1 a 2 ø 3 an 4 ø 5 a

1 Susan은 좋은 학생이다.
2 Charlie는 빨간 머리카락을 가지고 있다.
3 그녀는 사과를 먹고 있다.
4 내 형의 이름은 Joe이다.
5 Tony의 애완동물은 큰 뱀이다.

Comprehension Check

1 c 2 c 3 a True b False c True

1 Katie는 아파트에 살기 때문에 개를 가질 수 없다.
2 Katie의 엄마는 개털에 알레르기가 있다.
3 a Fred는 로봇개이다.
  b Fred는 큰 소리로 짖는다.
  c Fred는 털이 없다.

TRY IT

Haley, Luke

누가 로봇 애완동물이 필요한가?
Haley: 나의 가족은 개와 고양이를 좋아하지만, 내 남동생들은
    동물털에 알레르기가 있어.
Alex : 나의 가족은 큰 단독주택에 살아. 집에 큰 정원도 있어.
Luke : 나의 가족은 아파트에 살아. 내 이웃들은 소음을 싫어해.

STORY 02 PP.48~51

Words to Learn

grow: 자라다 smart: 똑똑한 smile: 웃다

greet: 반기다   guest: 손님

Grammar to Learn

그것은 큰 행복한 돼지이다!
사람들은 이 멋진 분홍 돼지를 사랑한다.

직독직해 P.49

Derek has / a pet pig, Esther.
Derek은 가졌다 / 애완돼지 Esther를
It was a small pink pig, / but it grew / so fast.
그것은 작은 분홍 돼지였다 / 그러나 그것은 자랐다 / 너무 빨리
It is 300kg / now!
그것은 300kg이다 / 지금
He loves it / very much.
그는 그것을 사랑한다 / 아주 많이
It is smart / and lovely.
그것은 똑똑하다 / 그리고 사랑스럽다
It goes / to the bathroom / by itself.
그것은 간다 / 화장실에 / 혼자서
It smiles / and greets guests.
그것은 웃는다 / 그리고 손님들을 반긴다
Some people / don't understand / him.
어떤 사람들은 / 이해하지 못한다 / 그를
They say / "Pigs are not pets!"
그들은 말한다 / 돼지들은 애완동물이 아니다
But this big clever pig is / his family.
그러나 그 크고 영리한 돼지는 ~이다 / 그의 가족

본문해석

Derek에게는 애완돼지 Esther가 있다.
그것은 작은 분홍색 돼지였지만, 너무 빠르게 자랐다.
지금 그것은 300kg이다!
그는 그것을 매우 사랑한다.
그것은 똑똑하고 사랑스럽다.
그것은 혼자서 화장실에 간다.
그것은 웃으며 손님을 맞이한다.
어떤 사람들은 그를 이해하지 못한다.
그들은 "돼지는 애완동물이 아니다!"라고 말한다.
그러나 이 크고 영리한 돼지는 그의 가족이다.

정답

MAIN IDEA

A Lovely Pet Pig

Word Check

1 ⓒ   2 ⓐ   3 ⓓ   4 ⓑ

Grammar Check

1 long blond   2 pretty pink   3 big brown

1 우리 선생님은 긴 금발머리를 가졌다.
2 그녀는 예쁜 분홍색 셔츠를 입고 있다.
3 나는 저 큰 갈색 곰인형을 원한다.

Comprehension Check

1 b   2 a False b True c True   3 a, b

1 Derek은 애완동물로 돼지를 가지고 있다.
2 a Esther는 지금 아주 작다.
  b Esther는 똑똑하다.
  c 어떤 사람들은 "돼지는 애완동물이 아니다!"라고 말한다.
3 Esther는 무엇을 할 수 있는가?

TRY IT

1) small   2) white   3) long   4) pink

이것은 내 애완동물 Joy이다.
그것은 작고 흰 토끼이다.
그것은 긴 분홍색 귀를 가졌다.
나는 내 애완동물을 사랑한다.

REVIEW TEST PP. 52~53

1 smile   2 greet   3 apartment   4 bark
5 smart   6 allergic   7 growing   8 neighbors
9 guests   10 loudly   11 short grey   12 a
beautiful white   13 a False b False   14 a, c

1   smile: 웃다
2   greet: 반기다
3   apartment: 아파트
4   bark: 짖다
5   smart: 똑똑한
6   Sue는 먼지에 알레르기가 있다.
7   내 개는 어리다. 그것은 아직도 자라고 있다.
8   내 이웃들은 애완동물이 없다.
9   파티에 많은 손님이 왔다.
10 교실에서 큰 소리로 말하지 마라.
11 그의 고양이는 짧은 회색 털을 가졌다.
12 나는 수족관에서 아름다운 흰 고래 한 마리를 보았다.
13 a Katie의 이웃들은 그녀의 개 때문에 화를 냈다.
     b Katie의 가족은 지금 애완동물이 없다.
14 Katie는 Fred가 짖지 않기[털이 없기] 때문에 이것을 데
     려왔다.

UNIT 05 CULTURE

STORY 01   PP.56~59

Words to Learn

first: 첫 번째의   sour: (맛이) 신   second: 두 번째의
beak: 부리   third: 세 번째의

Grammar to Learn

사람들은 나를 Jim이라고 부른다.
나의 엄마는 나를 왕자라고 부른다.
나의 친구들은 나를 원숭이라고 부른다.

직독직해   P.57

There are / three kinds of "kiwis" / in New Zealand.
~들이 있다 / 세 가지 종류의 키위가 / 뉴질랜드에는

The first kiwi is / a green, sweet and sour fruit.
첫 번째 키위는 ~이다 / 녹색의 달고 신 과일

The second kiwi is / a bird.
두 번째 키위는 ~이다 / 새

It has / a long beak and short wings.
이것은 가지고 있다 / 긴 부리와 짧은 날개를

It can't fly / and it makes a sound / like "kiwi."
이것은 날 수 없다 / 그리고 그것은 소리를 낸다 / '키위'와 비슷한

People call / it a kiwi.
사람들은 부른다 / 그것을 / 키위라고

The third kiwi means / the people / from New Zealand!
세 번째 키위는 의미한다 / 사람들을 / 뉴질랜드 출신의

We call / them / Kiwis.
우리는 부른다 / 그들을 / 키위라

본문해석

뉴질랜드에는 세 가지 종류의 키위가 있다.
첫 번째 키위는 녹색의 달고 신 과일이다.
두 번째 키위는 새이다.
그것은 긴 부리와 짧은 날개들을 가지고 있다.
그것은 날 수 없으며 '키위'와 비슷한 소리를 낸다.
사람들은 그것을 키위라고 부른다.
세 번째 키위는 뉴질랜드 출신의 사람들을 의미한다!
우리는 그들을 키위라고 부른다.

정답

MAIN IDEA

Kiwis in New Zealand

Word Check

1 ⓓ   2 ⓒ   3 ⓑ   4 ⓐ

Grammar Check

1 call the sour fruit a lemon
2 calls David a hero
3 call my sister a genius

1 사람들은 그 신 과일을 레몬이라고 부른다.
2 모든 사람들은 David를 영웅이라고 부른다.
3 나의 부모님은 내 여동생을 천재라고 부른다.

Comprehension Check

1 b   2 b   3 c

1 뉴질랜드에는 세 가지 종류의 키위가 있다.
2 키위새는 긴 부리와 짧은 날개를 가지고 있다.
3 세 번째 키위는 뉴질랜드 출신의 사람들을 의미한다.

TRY IT

1) New Zealand   2) kiwi   3) fly

Q: 그것은 어디에 사는가?
A: 그것은 뉴질랜드에 산다.
Q: 그것은 어떤 소리를 내는가?
A: 그것은 '키위'라는 소리를 낸다.
Q: 그것은 무엇을 할 수 없는가?
A: 그것은 날 수 없다.

STORY 02   PP.60~63

Words to Learn

invite: 초대하다   dessert: 디저트, 후식   tooth: 이
hold: (손에) 들다, 잡다   coin: 동전   tradition: 전통

Grammar to Learn

그것은 예쁜 인형이다.
정말 예쁜 인형이구나!

It was / New Year's Day.
~이었다 / 새해 첫날

Dan's Greek friend, / Irene, / invited him / to dinner.
Dan의 그리스 친구 / Irene은 / 그를 초대했다 / 저녁 식사에

They ate / Greek New Year's cake / for dessert.
그들은 먹었다 / 그리스 새해 케이크를 / 디저트로

"Ouch! My tooth! / What is this?" / Dan said.
"아 내 이 / 이게 무엇이지" / Dan이 말했다.

Irene laughed.
Irene은 웃었다.

Dan held / a coin / in his hand.
Dan은 들고 있었다 / 동전 하나를 / 그의 손에

"Congratulations!"
축하해

We put / a coin / into the cake.
우리는 넣는다 / 동전 하나를 / 그 케이크 안에

It means / "luck."
그것은 의미한다 / '행운'을

You found / it!
네가 찾았다 / 그것을

What a lucky boy!"
정말 운이 좋은 소년이구나

What an interesting tradition!
참 재미있는 전통이다

본문해석

새해 첫날이었다.
Dan의 그리스 친구 Irene은 그를 저녁 식사에 초대했다.
그들은 디저트로 그리스 새해 케이크를 먹었다.
"아야! 내 이! 이게 뭐지?" Dan이 말했다.
Irene은 웃었다. Dan은 그의 손에 동전을 하나 들고 있었다.
"축하해! 우리는 케이크에 동전을 하나 넣어. 그것은 '행운'을 의미해.
너가 그것을 발견한거야! 정말 운이 좋은 소년이구나!"
참 재미있는 전통이구나!

정답

MAIN IDEA

An Interesting Greek Tradition

Word Check

1 ⓑ   2 ⓐ   3 ⓓ   4 ⓒ

Grammar Check

1 an interesting book   2 cute puppies
3 a smart girl

1 정말 재미있는 책이구나!
2 정말 귀여운 강아지들이구나!
3 정말 똑똑한 소녀이구나!

Comprehension Check

1 b   2 b   3 a

1 새해 첫 날에 Dan은 Irene과 그리스 케이크를 먹었다.
2 전통에 따르면, 그리스 사람들은 그리스 케이크 안에 동전 하나를 넣는다.
3 누가 운이 좋은 사람인가?

TRY IT

1) invited   2) cake   3) coin   4) luck

Irene은 새해 첫 날에 Dan을 저녁 식사에 초대했다.
그들은 디저트로 그리스 케이크를 먹었다.
Dan은 케이크 안에서 동전을 하나 발견했다.
그 동전은 행운을 의미한다.

REVIEW TEST PP.64-65

1 tradition   2 first   3 second   4 sour   5 third
6 invited   7 tooth   8 held   9 coins   10 beak
11 What delicious cake   12 What an exciting trip   13 a False b True c True   14 c

1 tradition: 전통
2 first: 첫 번째의
3 second: 두 번째의
4 sour: (맛이) 신
5 third: 세 번째의
6 David는 파티에 나를 초대했다.
7 어제 Brian의 이가 아팠다.
8 Julie는 그녀의 손에 초록색 키위를 들고 있었다.
9 Linda는 동전 모으는 것을 좋아한다.
10 그 새는 짧은 부리를 가지고 있다.
11 정말 맛있는 케이크구나!
12 정말 신나는 여행이구나!
13 a Irene은 점심에 Dan을 초대했다.
   b Dan은 케이크 안에서 동전을 발견했다.
   c 케이크 안에 있는 동전은 '행운'을 의미한다.

UNIT 06 GOOD LUCK & BAD LUCK

STORY 01 PP.68~71

Words to Learn

symbol: 상징   around the world: 전 세계
wave: 흔들다   bill: 지폐   wallet: 지갑

Grammar to Learn

John은 미국 출신이다.
Sam은 가나 출신이다.
미나는 한국 출신이다.
진호는 영화관에 있다.
진호는 정문에 있다.

직독직해 P.69

Ron wants to be / the luckiest man / in the world.
Ron은 되고 싶어한다 / 가장 운이 좋은 사람이 / 세계에서
He collects / symbols of luck / from around the world.
그는 모은다 / 행운의 상징들을 / 전 세계로부터
He put / his cat doll / at the front door.
그는 놓았다 / 그의 고양이 인형을 / 현관에
It waves / its hand.
그것은 흔든다 / 그것의 손을
It is / from Japan.
그것은 왔다 / 일본에서
He carries / a two-dollar bill / in his wallet.
그는 가지고 다닌다 / 2달러 지폐를 / 그의 지갑 안에
It is / from the US.
그것은 왔다 / 미국에서
Now, / he wants / a white elephant.
이제 / 그는 원한다 / 흰 코끼리를
But / he can't bring it / from Thailand.
하지만 / 그는 그것을 가지고 올 수 없다 / 태국으로부터

본문해석

Ron은 세계에서 가장 운 좋은 사람이 되고 싶어한다.
그는 전 세계로부터 행운의 상징들을 모은다.
그는 그의 고양이 인형을 현관에 놓았다.
그것은 그것의 손을 흔든다.
그것은 일본에서 왔다.
그는 그의 지갑에 2달러 지폐를 가지고 다닌다.
그것은 미국에서 왔다.
이제 그는 흰 코끼리를 원한다.
하지만 그는 태국에서 그것을 가져올 수 없다.

정답

MAIN IDEA

Ron collects symbols of luck

Word Check

1 ⓓ   2 ⓐ   3 ⓒ   4 ⓑ

Grammar Check

1 from   2 at   3 from   4 at   5 at

1 이 인형은 멕시코에서 왔다.
2 Emily는 버스 정류장에 있다.
3 Brian과 Patrick은 캐나다 출신이다.
4 소라는 프랑스 음식점에 있다.
5 나의 엄마는 현관에 있다.

Comprehension Check

1 c   2 c   3 c

1 Ron은 세계에서 가장 운이 좋은 사람이 되고 싶어서 행운의 상징들을 모은다.
2 Ron은 그의 고양이 인형을 현관에 두었다.
3 Ron은 흰 코끼리를 가지고 있지 않다.

TRY IT

1) from   2) at   3) luck

나는 행운의 상징을 가지고 있다.
그것은 마트료시카 인형이다.
그것은 러시아에서 왔다.
나는 그것을 현관에 두었다.
그것은 나에게 행운을 가져다 줄 것이다.

STORY 02 PP.72~75

Words to Learn

mirror: 거울   broken: 깨진   fence: 울타리   sign: 징조
fail one's test: 시험을 못 보다, 낙제하다

Grammar to Learn

개가 침대 위에 있다.
햄스터는 상자 안에 있다.
두 마리의 고양이는 의자 아래에 있다.

직독직해 `p.73`

Today / I have a test.
오늘 / 나는 시험이 있다

This morning, / I looked at the clock / on the table.
오늘 아침 / 나는 시계를 봤다 / 테이블 위의

It was / 07:13.
이었다 / 7시 13분

The number 13! / Bad luck!
숫자 13 / 불운

I looked in the mirror / on the wall.
나는 거울을 들여다 봤다 / 벽에 있는

It was / broken!
그것은 ~이었다 / 깨진

More / bad luck!
더 많은 / 불운

Now, / I'm walking / to school.
이제 / 나는 걸어 가고 있다 / 학교로

I see a black cat / under a fence.
나는 검은 고양이를 본다 / 울타리 아래의

Three signs of bad luck!
불운의 세 가지 징조

I will / fail my test!
나는 ~할 것이다 / 시험을 못 보다

본문해석

오늘 나는 시험이 있다.
오늘 아침에 나는 테이블 위에 있는 시계를 보았다.
7시 13분이었다.
숫자 13! 불운이다!
나는 벽에 있는 거울을 보았다.
그것은 깨져있었다.
불운이 더해졌다!
이제 나는 학교에 걸어가고 있다.
나는 울타리 아래에 검은 고양이가 있다!
불운의 징조가 세 개나 된다!
나는 시험을 못 볼 것이다!

정답

MAIN IDEA

Three Signs of Bad Luck

Word Check

1 ⓑ   2 ⓒ   3 ⓐ   4 ⓓ

Grammar Check

1 on   2 in   3 on

1 시계가 벽 위에 있다.
2 거울이 상자 안에 있다.
3 검은 새가 울타리 위에 있다.

Comprehension Check

1 b   2 c   3 a

1 시계는 테이블 위에 있었고, 검은 고양이는 울타리 아래에 있었다.
2 소녀가 거울을 봤을 때 그것은 깨져있었다.
3 소녀는 세 가지 불운의 징조를 봐서 그녀는 시험을 못 볼 것이다.

TRY IT

1) 3   2) 1   3) 2   4) 4

1) 그 소녀는 검은 고양이를 봤다.
2) 그 소녀는 7시 13분에 시계를 봤다.
3) 그 소녀는 깨진 거울을 봤다.
4) 그 소녀는 시험에 대해 걱정했다.

REVIEW TEST `PP.76-77`

1 sign   2 around the world   3 fail one's test
4 mirror   5 fence   6 wallet   7 symbols
8 bills   9 broken   10 waved   11 a on b from
12 a on b under   13 b   14 a True b False
c False

1   sign: 징조
2   around the world: 전 세계
3   fail one's test: 시험을 못보다, 낙제하다
4   mirror: 거울
5   fence: 울타리
6   나는 나의 지갑에 그 돈을 넣었다.
7   Sally는 행운의 상징들을 많이 가지고 있다.
8   나는 나의 주머니에 지폐를 하나도 갖고 있지 않았다.
9   Dan은 깨진 접시를 닦았다.
10 나는 Tom에게 손을 흔들었다.
11 a 그는 침대 위에 있다.
    b 그는 미국 출신이다
12 a 열쇠는 의자 위에 있다.
    b 지갑은 의자 아래에 있다.
14 a 일본에서 온 그 고양이 인형은 그것의 손을 흔든다.
    b Ron은 태국에서 온 2달러 지폐를 갖고 있다.
    c Ron은 현재 흰 코끼리를 갖고 있다.

UNIT 07 TRAVEL THE WORLD

STORY 01 PP.80~83

Words to Learn

travel: 여행하다   careful: 조심스러운   rule: 규칙
subway: 지하철   flush the toilet: 변기 물을 내리다
pay a fine: 벌금을 내다

Grammar to Learn

당신은 조심해야 한다.
당신은 규칙을 지켜야 한다.
당신은 아무것도 먹어서는 안 된다.
당신은 아무것도 마셔서는 안 된다.

직독직해 P.81

남: I will travel / to Singapore.
　나는 여행을 갈 것이다 / 싱가포르로
　I'm / excited.
　나는 ~이다 / 신이 난

여: Wow! / But you should / be careful.
　와 / 하지만 너는 ~해야 한다 / 조심하다

남: Why?
　왜

여: Some rules / there / are different from / Korea.
　몇 가지 규칙 / 그곳의 / ~과 다르다 / 한국

남: What are / their rules?
　무엇인가 / 그들의 규칙이

여: You should not / eat anything / on the subway.
　너는 ~해서는 안 된다 / 아무것도 먹어서는 / 지하철을 타고
　And you should not / feed birds / in the park.
　그리고 너는 ~해서는 안 된다 / 새에게 먹이를 주어서는 /
　공원에서

남: Anything / else?
　다른 것은 / 그 외에

여: Flush the toilet / after you use it / or / you
　will have to / pay a fine.
　변기 물을 내려라 / 그것을 사용한 후에 / 아니면 / 너는
　~할 것이다. / 벌금을 내야

남: Thanks!
　고맙다

본문해석

남: 나는 싱가포르로 여행갈 거야. 나는 신나.
여: 와! 하지만 너는 조심해야 해.

남: 왜?
여: 거기 몇 가지 규칙이 한국과 다르거든.
남: 그들의 규칙이 무엇인데?
여: 너는 지하철을 타고 아무것도 먹으면 안 돼. 그리고 너
　는 공원에서 새에게 먹이를 줘서는 안 돼.
남: 그 밖에 다른 것은?
여: 변기를 사용한 후 물을 반드시 내려, 그렇지 않으면 너
　는 벌금을 내야해.
남: 고마워!

정답

MAIN IDEA

Some Rules in Singapore

Word Check

1 ⓑ   2 ⓓ   3 ⓐ   4 ⓒ

Grammar Check

1 should not eat   2 should be
3 should not waste

1 당신은 도서관에서 먹으면 안 된다.
2 당신은 교실에서 조용히 해야만 한다.
3 당신은 물을 낭비해서는 안 된다.

Comprehension Check

1 a   2 b   3 b

1 소년은 왜 싱가포르에 가는가?
2 싱가포르에서는 당신은 지하철에서 아무것도 먹어서는 안 된다.
3 싱가포르에서는 당신은 공원에서 새에게 먹이를 주면 안 된다.

TRY IT

1) should not feed monkeys
2) should not chew gum

싱가포르의 다른 규칙들!
당신은 지하철에서 담배를 피워서는 안 된다.
당신은 동물원에서 원숭이들에게 먹이를 주어서는 안 된다.
당신은 길에서 껌을 씹어서는 안 된다.

STORY 02 PP.84~87

Words to Learn

be made of: ~로 만들어지다   worry: 걱정하다

sleeping bag: 침낭   fun: 재미   afternoon: 오후

Grammar to Learn

그녀는 스키 타러 갈 것이다. / 그는 캠핑하러 갈 것이다.

직독직해 `P.85`

Mom: Look, / Tom!
보렴 / Tom

Everything / in this hotel / is made of / ice / — tables, chairs and beds!
모든 것들은 / 이 호텔의 / ~로 만들어지다 / 얼음 / 테이블, 의자 그리고 침대

Tom: Ice beds? / Mom, / we're going to / be cold!
얼음 침대 / 엄마 / 우리는 ~할 것이다 / 춥다

Mom: Don't worry.
걱정하지 마라

We'll sleep / in very warm sleeping bags.
우리는 잘 것이다 / 매우 따뜻한 침낭 안에서

Tom: Oh, good! / What are we going to do / tomorrow?
오, 좋아요 / 우리는 무엇을 하나요 / 내일

Mom: After / we have a breakfast, / we'll go ice skating!
~한 후에 / 아침을 먹은 / 우리는 아이스 스케이트 타러 갈 것이다

Tom: Sounds like / fun!
~처럼 들리다 / 재미

Mom: In the afternoon, / we'll go ice fishing.
오후에 / 우리는 얼음 낚시하러 갈 것이다

본문해석

Mom: 이것 봐, Tom!
이 호텔에 있는 모든 것이 얼음으로 만들어져 있어. 테이블, 의자, 침대도!

Tom: 얼음 침대라고요? 엄마, 우리는 추울 거예요!

Mom: 걱정하지마.
우리는 매우 따뜻한 침낭 안에서 잘 거야.

Tom: 오, 다행이네요! 저희 내일은 무엇을 할 예정인가요?

Mom: 우리는 아침을 먹은 후에 아이스 스케이트 타러 갈 거야!

Tom: 재미있게 들리네요!

Mom: 오후에, 우리는 얼음 낚시하러 갈 거야!

정답

MAIN IDEA

An Ice Hotel

Word Check

1 ⓐ   2 ⓒ   3 ⓓ   4 ⓑ

Grammar Check

1 go swimming   2 go shopping   3 go skiing

Peter는 내일 하이킹하러 가기를 원한다.
1 Cindy는 다음 주에 수영하러 갈 것이다.
2 오후에 쇼핑하러 가자.
3 나는 이번 주말에 스키 타러 가고 싶다.

Comprehension Check

1 a   2 c   3 b

1 이 호텔에서는 테이블, 의자, 그리고 침대가 얼음으로 만들어져 있다.
2 Tom과 그의 엄마는 침낭에서 잠을 잘 것이다.
3 Tom과 그의 엄마는 내일 오후에 얼음 낚시하러 갈 것이다.

TRY IT

1) 2   2) 3   3) 1

내일의 계획
그들은 아이스 스케이트 타러 갈 것이다.
그들은 얼음 낚시하러 갈 것이다.
그들은 아침을 먹을 것이다.

REVIEW TEST `PP.88-89`

1 subway   2 sleeping bag   3 flush the toilet
4 be made of   5 afternoon   6 fun   7 travel
8 careful   9 worry   10 rules   11 should
12 should not   13 b   14 a False b False

1 subway: 지하철
2 sleeping bag: 침낭
3 flush the toilet: 변기 물을 내리다
4 be made of: ~로 만들어지다
5 afternoon: 오후
6 우리는 내일 즐거운 시간을 보낼 것이다.
7 Joe는 제주도로 여행을 갈 것이다.
8 당신은 운전할 때 조심해야 한다.
9 내일 시험에 대해 걱정하지 마.
10 모든 나라는 다른 규칙들을 가지고 있다.
11 당신은 빨간불에 멈춰야 한다.
12 당신은 박물관에서 아무 것도 먹어서는 안 된다.
13 그 소년은 싱가포르로 여행을 갈 것이기 때문에 신이 난다.
14 a 싱가포르의 규칙은 한국의 것과 같다.
b 사람들은 싱가포르의 지하철에서 음식을 먹을 수 있다.

UNIT 08 HOW STRANGE!

STORY 01 PP.92~95

Words to Learn

win: 우승하다　try one's best: 최선을 다하다
terrible: 심한, 지독한　wear: 입다　playground: 운동장
step: 밟다

Grammar to Learn

그는 어젯밤에 영화를 봤다.
그녀는 어젯밤에 영화를 보지 않았다.

직독직해 P.93

Last week, / Tim won / the Smelliest Shoes Contest.
지난주에 / Tim은 우승했다 / 가장 냄새 나는 신발 대회에서
He tried his best / to make his shoes smell terrible.
그는 최선을 다했다 / 그의 신발이 지독한 냄새가 나게 만들기 위해
He wore them / everywhere / without socks / —
inside the house, / at the playground.
그는 그것들을 신었다 / 모든 곳에서 / 양말 없이 / 집 안에서 /
운동장에서
He stepped in / dog-doo.
그는 ~을 밟았다 / 개똥
He / also / didn't wash his feet! / Yuck!
그는 / 또한 / 발을 씻지 않았다 / 윽
He was happy / to win.
그는 행복했다 / 우승해서
But his friends didn't play / with him / anymore
/ because of / his smelly shoes.
하지만 그의 친구들은 놀지 않았다 / 그와 함께 / 더 이상 / ~
때문에 / 그의 냄새 나는 신발

본문해석

지난주에 Tim은 가장 냄새 나는 신발 대회에서 우승했다.
그는 그의 신발이 지독한 냄새가 나게 만들기 위해 최선을
다했다.
그는 그것들을 양말을 신지 않고 어디에서나 신었다.
집 안에서, 운동장에서도 말이다.
그는 개똥을 밟았다.
그는 또한 그의 발을 씻지 않았다! 윽!
그는 우승해서 행복했다.
하지만 그의 냄새 나는 신발 때문에 그의
친구들은 더 이상 그와 함께 놀지 않았다.

정답

MAIN IDEA

Tim won the Smelliest Shoes Contes

Word Check

1 ⓑ　2 ⓓ　3 ⓐ　4 ⓒ

Grammar Check

1 didn't step　2 didn't wash　3 didn't try

1 당신은 어제 나의 발을 밟지 않았다.
2 그는 오늘 아침에 세수를 하지 않았다.
3 나는 시험에서 최선을 다하지 않았다.

Comprehension Check

1 c　2 b　3 a

1 Tim은 무엇을 했는가?
2 Tim은 대회에서 우승해서 행복했다.
3 Tim의 친구들은 그의 냄새 나는 신발 때문에 그와 함께 놀지
않았다.

TRY IT

1) didn't wear　2) stepped　3) didn't wash

Q: 가장 냄새 나는 신발 대회의 우승자는 누구인가?
A: Tim이 우승자였다.
Q: 우승자는 대회에서 우승하기 위해 무엇을 했었나?
A: 그는 양말을 신지 않았다.
　그는 개똥을 밟았다.
　그는 그의 발을 씻지 않았다.

STORY 02 PP.96~99

Words to Learn

stick: 붙이다　behavior: 행동　colorful: (색이) 다채로운,
알록달록한　cover: 덮다　start: 시작되다

Grammar to Learn

그 기차는 얼마나 긴가요? / 그 기차는 얼마나 높은가요?
얼마나 많은 사과가 있나요?

직독직해 P.97

Come here!
여기로 와라

Stick your gum / on the wall!
네 껌을 붙여라 / 벽 위에

It is not / bad behavior.
이것은 ~이 아니다 / 나쁜 행동

Colorful gum covers / the wall!
알록달록한 껌이 덮는다 / 벽을

Q: Where is / the wall?
어디에 있는가 / 그 벽은

A: It is / in California.
그것은 있다 / 캘리포니아에

Q: How long / is the wall?
얼마나 긴 / 그 벽은

A: It is / 20 meters long.
그것은 ~이다 / 길이가 20m

Q: How high / is the wall?
얼마나 높은 / 그 벽은?

A: It is / 4.5 meters high.
그것은 ~이다 / 높이가 4.5m

Q: When / did it start?
언제 / 그것은 시작되었는가?

A: It started / about 50 years ago.
그것은 시작되었다 / 약 50년 전에

본문해석

여기에 오세요! 벽에 당신의 껌을 붙이세요!
그것은 나쁜 행동이 아닙니다.
알록달록한 껌이 벽을 덮고 있습니다!

Q: 그 벽은 어디에 있나요?
A: 그것은 캘리포니아에 있습니다.
Q: 그 벽은 얼마나 긴가요?
A: 그것은 길이가 20m입니다.
Q: 그 벽은 얼마나 높은가요?
A: 그것은 높이가 4.5m입니다.
Q: 그것은 언제 시작되었나요?
A: 그것은 약 50년 전에 시작되었습니다.

정답

MAIN IDEA

Colorful Gum Wall

Word Check

1 ⓑ   2 ⓐ   3 ⓓ   4 ⓒ

Grammar Check

1 How high   2 How long   3 How many
4 How long   5 How high

1 Q: 이 나무는 얼마나 높은가요?
  A: 그것은 높이가 3m입니다.
2 Q: 그 자는 얼마나 긴가요?
  A: 그것은 길이가 50cm입니다.
3 Q: 당신의 가방에 얼마나 많은 책이 있나요?
  A: 세 권의 책이 내 가방에 있어요.
4 Q: 그 강은 얼마나 긴가요?
  A: 그것은 481km입니다.
5 Q: 그 산은 얼마나 높은가요?
  A: 그것은 8,848m입니다.

Comprehension Check

1 b   2 b   3 a True b True c False

1 사람들은 벽에 그들의 껌을 붙일 수 있다.
2 껌 벽은 길이가 20m이고 높이가 4.5m이다
3 a 벽은 알록달록한 껌들로 덮여 있다.
  b 그 벽은 캘리포니아에 있다.
  c 사람들은 약 40년 전에 껌을 붙이기 시작했다.

TRY IT

1) Where   2) How high   3) When

Q: 에펠탑은 어디에 있나요?   A: 그것은 파리에 있습니다.
Q: 그것은 얼마나 높은가요?   A: 그것은 높이가 324m입니다.
Q: 그것은 언제 지어졌나요?
A: 그것은 약 120년 전에 지어졌습니다.

REVIEW TEST PP. 100~101

1 cover   2 start   3 stick   4 try one's best
5 step   6 Colorful   7 behavior   8 terrible
9 won   10 wear   11 didn't wear   12 How
long   13 b   14 a False b False c True

1   cover: 덮다   2   start: 시작하다
3   stick: 붙이다   4   try one's best: 최선을 다하다
5   step: 밟다
6   알록달록한 꽃들이 테이블을 덮고 있다.
7   거짓말을 하는 것은 나쁜 행동이다.
8   이 음식은 지독한 냄새가 난다.
9   내가 가장 좋아하는 선수가 경주에서 우승했다.
10 John의 개는 옷을 입는 것을 좋아한다.
11 그는 어제 양말을 신지 않았다.
12 Q: 그 다리는 얼마나 긴가요?
    A: 그것은 길이가 69.5km입니다.
14 a Tim은 양말을 신고 운동장에 갔다.
    b Tim은 대회에서 우승해서 행복하지 않았다.
    c Tim의 친구들은 그의 냄새 나는 신발을 좋아하지 않았다.

지은이

NE능률 영어교육연구소

NE능률 영어교육연구소는 혁신적이며 효율적인 영어 교재를 개발하고
영어 학습의 질을 한 단계 높이고자 노력하는 NE능률의 연구조직입니다.

리딩버디 2

펴 낸 이	주민홍
펴 낸 곳	서울특별시 마포구 월드컵북로 396(상암동) 누리꿈스퀘어 비즈니스타워 10층
	(주)NE능률 (우편번호 03925)
펴 낸 날	2016년 1월 5일 개정판 제1쇄
	2023년 4월 15일 제15쇄
전 화	02 2014 7114
팩 스	02 3142 0356
홈페이지	www.neungyule.com
등록번호	제 1-68호
I S B N	979-11-253-0970-3 63740
정 가	10,000원

NE능률

고객센터

교재 내용 문의 : contact.nebooks.co.kr (별도의 가입 절차 없이 작성 가능)
제품 구매, 교환, 불량, 반품 문의 : 02-2014-7114
☎ 전화문의는 본사 업무시간 중에만 가능합니다.

NE능률 교재 MAP

독해

아래 교재 MAP을 참고하여 본인의 현재 혹은 목표 수준에 따라 교재를 선택하세요.
NE능률 교재들과 함께 영어실력을 쑥쑥~ 올려보세요!
MP3 등 교재 부가 학습 서비스 및 자세한 교재 정보는 www.nebooks.co.kr 에서 확인하세요.

초1-2
초등영어 리딩이 된다 Start 1
초등영어 리딩이 된다 Start 2
초등영어 리딩이 된다 Start 3
초등영어 리딩이 된다 Start 4

초3
리딩버디 1

초3-4
리딩버디 2
초등영어 리딩이 된다 Basic 1
초등영어 리딩이 된다 Basic 2
초등영어 리딩이 된다 Basic 3
초등영어 리딩이 된다 Basic 4

초4-5
리딩버디 3
주니어 리딩튜터 스타터 1

초5-6
초등영어 리딩이 된다 Jump 1
초등영어 리딩이 된다 Jump 2
초등영어 리딩이 된다 Jump 3
초등영어 리딩이 된다 Jump 4
주니어 리딩튜터 스타터 2

초6-예비중
1316팬클럽 독해 1
주니어 리딩튜터 1
Junior Reading Expert 1
Reading Forward Basic 1

중1
주니어 리딩튜터 2
Junior Reading Expert 2
Reading Forward Basic 2
열중 16강 독해+문법 1
Reading Inside Starter

중1-2
1316팬클럽 독해 2
주니어 리딩튜터 3
정말 기특한 구문독해 입문
Junior Reading Expert 3
Reading Forward Intermediate 1
열중 16강 독해+문법 2
Reading Inside 1

중2-3
1316팬클럽 독해 3
주니어 리딩튜터 4
정말 기특한 구문독해 기본
Junior Reading Expert 4
Reading Forward Intermediate 2
Reading Inside 2

중3
리딩튜터 입문
정말 기특한 구문독해 완성
Reading Forward Advanced 1
열중 16강 독해+문법 3
Reading Inside 3

중3-예비고
Reading Expert 1
리딩튜터 기본
Reading Forward Advanced 2

고1
빠바 기초세우기
리딩튜터 실력
Reading Expert 2
TEPS BY STEP G+R Basic

고1-2
빠바 구문독해
리딩튜터 수능 PLUS
Reading Expert 3

고2-3, 수능 실전
빠바 유형독해
빠바 종합실전편
Reading Expert 4
TEPS BY STEP G+R 1

고3 이상, 수능 고난도
Reading Expert 5
능률 고급영문독해

수능 이상/
토플 80-89 ·
텝스 600-699점
ADVANCED Reading Expert 1
TEPS BY STEP G+R 2
RADIX TOEFL Blue Label Reading 1,2

수능 이상/
토플 90-99 ·
텝스 700-799점
ADVANCED Reading Expert 2
RADIX TOEFL Black Label Reading 1

수능 이상/
토플 100 ·
텝스 800점 이상
RADIX TOEFL Black Label Reading 2
TEPS BY STEP G+R 3

초등학생의 영어 친구

리딩버디
WORKBOOK

2

HA! HA! HA!

OMG!!!

NE능률

초등학생의 영어 친구

리딩버디

WORKBOOK

2

[1~2] Look at the pictures and choose the right words.

cucumber   recipe

1   2

_____   _____

[3~5] Choose and write the right words three times.

add   carrot   follow

3   당근   _____   _____   _____

4   따라 하다   _____   _____   _____

5   더하다   _____   _____   _____

[6~8] Match the sentence parts and write the complete sentences.

6   She   •   • ⓐ had a ticket for a robot show.

7   The robot •   • ⓑ added salt to the food.

8   I   •   • ⓒ used a knife.

6   _____

7   _____

8   _____

[9~11] Write the words in the correct order.

9   어제 나는 영어를 열심히 공부했다. (hard / I / studied / English)

→ Yesterday, _____.

10   오늘 아침에 그는 당근과 감자를 썰었다. (cut / he / carrots and potatoes)

→ This morning, _____.

11   Kira는 로봇전시회에 갔다. (Kira / went to / a robot show)

→ _____

[1~3] Look at the pictures and write the words correctly.

1

ahrd

_____

2

natrsotau

_____

3

caekagp

_____

[4~6] Choose and write the right words three times.

| pour | vegetable | microwave |

4 채소   _____   _____   _____

5 붓다   _____   _____   _____

6 전자레인지   _____   _____   _____

[7~9] Match the sentence parts and write the complete sentences.

7　　Why does she　•　•　ⓐ eat?

8　　What does he　•　•　ⓑ bake it?

9　　How do astronauts　•　•　ⓒ cook their food?

7 _____

8 _____

9 _____

[10~12] Write the words in the correct order.

10　그가 언제 그것을 먹나요? (eat it / he / when / does)

　➡ _____

11　그녀는 어디서 그것을 굽나요? (she / where / it / does / bake)

　➡ _____

12　그것을 누가 먹나요? (it / who / eats)

　➡ _____

[1~2] Look at the pictures and choose the right words.

celebrate   chocolate

1

_____

2

_____

[3~5] Choose and write the right words three times.

each other   interesting   the United States

3   미국   _____   _____   _____

4   흥미로운   _____   _____   _____

5   서로   _____   _____   _____

[6~8] Match the sentence parts and write the complete sentences.

6   Valentines's Day is •   • ⓐ on Valentine's Day.

7   Image of a girl   She gets candy •   • ⓑ in February.

8   Image of a boy   He gets chocolate •   • ⓒ on White Day.

6   _____

7   _____

8   _____

[9~11] Write the words in the correct order.

9   내 생일은 11월이다. (my birthday / November / in / is)

→   _____

10   크리스마스는 12월이다. (December / in / Christmas / is)

→   _____

11   우리는 설날에 떡국을 먹는다. (we / New Year's Day / on / tteokguk / eat)

→   _____

[1~2] Look at the pictures and write the words correctly.

1

crhi

_____

2

elthate

_____

[3~5] Choose and write the right words three times.

	choose	several	pick up

3 고르다 _____ _____ _____

4 몇몇의 _____ _____ _____

5 집어 들다 _____ _____ _____

[6~8] Match the sentence parts and write the complete sentences.

6      The mike means •

                                                 • ⓐ an athlete.

7      The money means •

                                               • ⓑ a rich person.

8      The ball means •

                                               • ⓒ a singer.

6 _____

7 _____

8 _____

[9~11] Write the words in the correct order.

9   그 공은 빨간색이다. (is / red / the ball)

   ➡ _____

10   그 소녀는 아름다웠다. (beautiful / the girl / was)

   ➡ _____

11   그 쿠키들은 맛있었다. (delicious / were / the cookies)

   ➡ _____

[1~2] Look at the pictures and choose the right words.

climb   prison

1

_____

2

_____

[3~5] Choose and write the right words three times.

         delivery   fast   peace

3 배달   _____   _____   _____

4 평화   _____   _____   _____

5 빠르게   _____   _____   _____

[6~8] Match the sentence parts and write the complete sentences.

6   She will be   •   • ⓐ a window cleaner.

7   He will be   •   • ⓑ a doctor.

8   He will be   •   • ⓒ a delivery man.

6 _____

7 _____

8 _____

[9~11] Write the words in the correct order.

9 나는 택시 운전사가 될 것이다. (will / a taxi driver / be / I)

→ _____

10 그녀는 자동차를 운전할 것이다. (drive / a car / will / she)

→ _____

11 나는 아픈 사람들을 도울 것이다. (sick / will / I / people / help)

→ _____

[1~3] Look at the pictures and write the words correctly.

1	2	3
apce	**ctatak**	**rstnog**
_____	_____	_____

[4~6] Choose and write the right words three times.

	resemble	be afraid of	train

4 닮다   _____   _____   _____

5 단련하다   _____   _____   _____

6 두려워하다   _____   _____   _____

[7~8] Match the sentence parts and write the complete sentences.

7      Superman is   •   • ⓐ but he has a car.

8   Batman can't fly,   •   • ⓑ fast and strong.

7   _____

8   _____

[9~11] Write the words in the correct order.

9   Bruce는 강하고 용감하다. (is / strong / brave / and / Bruce)

→ _____

10   나는 박쥐를 좋아하지만, Joe는 그것들을 좋아하지 않는다.

(doesn't like / Joe / I / bats, / but / them / like)

→ _____

11   배트맨과 슈퍼맨은 히어로들이다. (heroes / and / Batman / are / Superman)

→ _____

[1~2] Look at the pictures and choose the right words.

apartment   bark

1   2

_____   _____

[3~5] Choose and write the right words three times.

allergic   neighbor   loudly

3   이웃   _____   _____   _____

4   큰 소리로   _____   _____   _____

5   알레르기가 있는 _____   _____   _____

[6~7] Match the sentence parts and write the complete sentences.

6   She is   •   •   ⓐ Bob.

7   Its name is   •   •   ⓑ a student.

6   _____

7   _____

[8~10] Write the words in the correct order.

8   그것은 사랑스러운 애완동물이다. (lovely pet / it / a / is)

→   _____

9   내 남동생의 이름은 Joe이다. (my brother's name / Joe / is)

→   _____

10   Tony의 애완동물은 큰 뱀이다. (big snake / Tony's pet / is / a)

→   _____

UNIT 04 ☆ MY PET STORY 02

[1~2] Look at the pictures and write the words correctly.

1

imles

_____

2

tegre

_____

[3~5] Choose and write the right words three times.

	grow	guest	smart
3 똑똑한	_____	_____	_____
4 손님	_____	_____	_____
5 자라다	_____	_____	_____

16

[6~8] Match the sentence parts and write the complete sentences.

6   She is wearing   •   • ⓐ a pretty pink shirt.

7   My teacher has   •   • ⓑ the big brown teddy bear.

8   I want   •   • ⓒ long blond hair.

6 _____

7 _____

8 _____

[9~11] Write the words in the correct order.

9   사람들은 이 멋진 분홍 돼지를 사랑한다. (this / love / people / wonderful / pig / pink)

→ _____

10 그것은 큰 행복한 돼지이다. (big / it / pig / is / a / happy)

→ _____

11 그것은 작은 흰 토끼이다. (white / it / a / is / rabbit / small)

→ _____

UNIT 05 ☆ CULTURE STORY 01

[1~2] Look at the pictures and choose the right words.

sour　　　beak

1

____

2

____

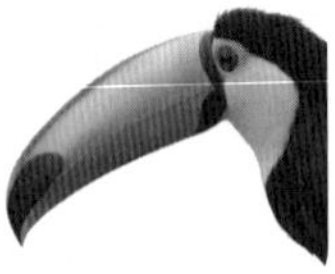

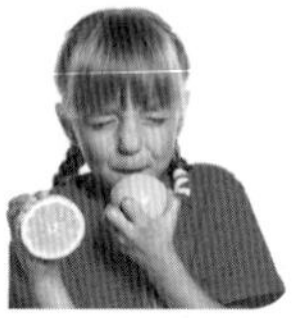

[3~5] Choose and write the right words three times.

third　　　first　　　second

3 첫 번째의 ______________ ______________ ______________

4 두 번째의 ______________ ______________ ______________

5 세 번째의 ______________ ______________ ______________

[6~8] Match the sentence parts and write the complete sentences.

6   My mother calls •　　　• ⓐ me Jim.

7   My friends call •　　　• ⓑ me a prince.

8   People call •　　　• ⓒ me monkey.

6 _____

7 _____

8 _____

[9~11] Write the words in the correct order.

9 우리는 David를 영웅이라고 부른다. (a hero/ call / David / we)

   → _____

10 사람들은 그 새를 키위라고 부른다. (call / people / a kiwi / the bird)

   → _____

11 사람들은 그 신 과일을 레몬이라고 부른다. (the sour fruit / call / a lemon / people)

   → _____

[1~3] Look at the pictures and write the words correctly.

1

odhl

_____

2

aditotrin

_____

3

hotot

_____

[4~6] Choose and write the right words three times.

invite   coin   dessert

4   초대하다   _____ _____ _____

5   디저트, 후식   _____ _____ _____

6   동전   _____ _____ _____

7   정말 운이 좋은 소년이구나!

What (a lucky / lucky a) boy!

➡ _____

8   정말 재미있는 전통이구나!

(What / How) an interesting tradition!

➡ _____

9   정말 신나는 여행이구나!

What (an exciting / exciting) trip!

➡ _____

10 정말 예쁜 인형이구나! (a / pretty / what / doll)

➡ _____

11 정말 재미있는 책이구나! (interesting / an / book / what)

➡ _____

12 정말 귀여운 강아지들이구나! (cute / puppies / what)

➡ _____

[1~2] Look at the pictures and choose the right words.

wave   symbol

1   2

_____   _____

[3~5] Choose and write the right words three times.

bill   wallet   around the world

3   지폐   _____   _____   _____

4   지갑   _____   _____   _____

5   전 세계   _____   _____   _____

[6~7] Match the sentence parts and write the complete sentences.

6      Jinho is •   • ⓐ from Korea.

7   Mina is •   • ⓑ at the theater.

6   _____

7   _____

[8~10] Write the words in the correct order.

8   John은 미국 출신이다. (the US / John / from / is)

→   _____

9   그는 현관에 고양이 인형을 놓았다. (at / he / the cat doll / the front door /put)

→   _____

10 그는 태국으로부터 코끼리를 가져올 수 없다.

(can't / from / bring / he / Thailand / an elephant)

→   _____

[1~2] Look at the pictures and write the words correctly.

1

ecnfe

_____

2

orkenb

_____

[3~5] Choose and write the right words three times.

	mirror	fail one's test	sign

3 징조 _____ _____ _____

4 시험을 못 보다 _____ _____ _____

5 거울 _____ _____ _____

[6~8] Match the sentence parts and write the complete sentences.

6   The clock is   •   •   ⓐ in the box.

7   The bird is   •   •   ⓑ on the fence.

8   The mirror is   •   •   ⓒ on the wall.

6   _____

7   _____

8   _____

[9~11] Write the words in the correct order.

9   열쇠는 의자 위에 있다. (is / a key / the chair / on)

→   _____

10   지갑은 의자 아래에 있다. (the chair / is / a wallet /under)

→   _____

11   시계는 테이블 위에 있었다. (on /was /the table /the clock)

→   _____

[1~3] Look at the pictures and choose the right words.

careful   flush the toilet   subway

1

_____

2

_____

3

_____

[4~6] Choose and write the right words three times.

rule   pay a fine   travel

4   규칙   _____   _____   _____

5   여행하다   _____   _____   _____

6   벌금을 내다   _____   _____   _____

[7~9] Match the sentence parts and write the complete sentences.

7   You should •   • ⓐ be quiet in the classroom.

8   You should •   • ⓑ not waste water.

9   You should •   • ⓒ not eat anything in the library.

7 _____

8 _____

9 _____

[10~12] Write the words in the correct order.

10 당신은 조심해야만 한다. (should / you / careful / be)

➡ _____

11 당신은 새에게 먹이를 줘서는 안 된다. (you / feed / not / should / birds)

➡ _____

12 당신은 담배를 피워서는 안 된다. (not / smoke / should / you)

➡ _____

[1~2] Look at the pictures and write the words correctly.

1

nfu

_____

2

orwry

_____

[3~5] Choose and write the right words three times.

| be made of | sleeping bag | afternoon |

3 침낭 _____ _____ _____

4 오후 _____ _____ _____

5 ~로 만들어지다 _____ _____ _____

[6~8] Match the sentence parts and write the complete sentences.

6      Let's   •   • ⓐ go shopping.

7   They want to •   • ⓑ go swimming.

8      They will   •   • ⓒ go hiking.

6   _____

7   _____

8   _____

[9~11] Write the words in the correct order.

9   그녀는 스키 타러 갈 것이다. (skiing / she / will / go)

    ➜ _____

10 그는 캠핑하러 갈 것이다. (go / will / camping / he)

    ➜ _____

11 그들은 얼음 낚시하러 갈 것이다. (they / ice fishing / will / go)

    ➜ _____

[1~3] Look at the pictures and choose the right words.

wear	terrible	try one's best

1 _____

2 _____

3 _____

[4~6] Choose and write the right words three times.

playground	win	step

4 밟다   _____   _____   _____

5 우승하다   _____   _____   _____

6 운동장   _____   _____   _____

[7~9] Choose the correct word and write the complete sentence.

7　그는 그의 발을 씻지 않았다.

He (wasn't / didn't) wash his feet.

➡ _____

8　그녀는 지난주에 대회에서 우승하지 않았다.

Ellis (doesn't / didn't) win the contest last week.

➡ _____

9　너는 어제 내 발을 밟지 않았다.

You (don't / didn't) step on my foot yesterday.

➡ _____

[10~12] Write the words in the correct order.

10　그는 양말을 신지 않았다. (didn't / he / socks / wear)

➡ _____

11　Tim의 친구들은 그와 함께 놀지 않았다. (him / play with / Tim's friends /didn't)

➡ _____

12　그들은 그의 냄새 나는 신발을 좋아하지 않았다.

(they / didn't / his smelly shoes / like)

➡ _____

[1~2] Look at the pictures and write the words correctly.

1

vecro

_____

2

itcsk

_____

[3~5] Choose and write the right words three times.

	behavior	start	colorful

3 알록달록한 _____ _____ _____

4 행동 _____ _____ _____

5 시작되다 _____ _____ _____

[6~8] Choose the correct word and write the complete sentence.

6   Q: (How high / How long) is the bridge?

    A: It is 60 kilometers long.

    ➡ _____

7   Q: (How many / How high) is this tree?

    A: It is 4 meters high.

    ➡ _____

8   Q: (How many / How long) books are in your bag?

    A: Three books are in my bag.

    ➡ _____

[9~11] Write the words in the correct order.

9   그 기차는 얼마나 높은가요? (the train / high / is / how)

    ➡ _____

10   거기에 사과가 몇 개 있나요? (many / how / are / apples / there)

    ➡ _____

11   그 자는 얼마나 긴가요? (the ruler / how / long / is)

    ➡ _____

 **☆ 정답 ☆**

UNIT 01 ☆
FOOD & COOKING

STORY 01 PP.2~3

1 recipe 2 cucumber 3 carrot 4 follow
5 add 6 ⓐ She had a ticket for a robot
show. 7 ⓒ The robot used a knife. 8 ⓑ
I added salt to the food. 9 I studied
English hard 10 he cut carrots and
potatoes 11 Kira went to a robot show.

STORY 02 PP.4~5

1 hard 2 astronaut 3 package
4 vegetable 5 pour 6 microwave 7 ⓑ
Why does she bake it? 8 ⓐ What does
he eat? 9 ⓒ How do astronauts cook
their food? 10 When does he eat it?
11 Where does she bake it? 12 Who eats
it?

UNIT 02 ☆
SPECIAL DAYS

STORY 01 PP.6~7

1 celebrate 2 chocolate 3 the United
States 4 interesting 5 each other
6 ⓑ Valentine's Day is in February. 7 ⓒ
She gets candy on White Day. 8 ⓐ He
gets chocolate on Valentine's Day 9 My
birthday is in November. 10 Christmas
is in December. 11 We eat tteokguk on
New Year's Day.

STORY 02 PP.8~9

1 rich 2 athlete 3 choose 4 several
5 pick up 6 ⓒ The mike means a singer.
7 ⓑ The money means a rich person.
8 ⓐ The ball means an athlete.

9 The ball is red. 10 The girl was
beautiful. 11 The cookies were delicious

UNIT 03 ☆
SUPERHEROES

STORY 01 PP.10~11

1 climb 2 prison 3 delivery 4 peace
5 fast 6 ⓑ She will be a doctor. 7 ⓒ He
will be a delivery man. 8 ⓐ He will be a
window cleaner. 9 I will be a taxi driver.
10 She will drive a car. 11 I will help sick
people.

STORY 02 PP.12~13

1 cape 2 attack 3 strong 4 resemble
5 train 6 be afraid of 7 ⓑ Superman is
fast and strong. 8 ⓐ Batman can't fly,
but he has a car. 9 Bruce is strong and
brave. 10 I like bats, but Joe doesn't like
them. 11 Batman and Superman are
heroes.

UNIT 04 ☆
MY PET

STORY 01 PP.14~15

1 apartment 2 bark 3 neighbor
4 loudly 5 allergic 6 ⓑ She is a student.
7 ⓐ Its name is Bob. 8 It is a lovely pet.
9 My brother's name is Joe. 10 Tony's
pet is a big snake.

STORY 02 PP.16~17

1 smile 2 greet 3 smart 4 guest 5 grow
6 ⓐ She is wearing a pretty pink shirt. 7 ⓒ
My teacher has long blond hair. 8 ⓑ I want
the big brown teddy bear. 9 People love
this wonderful pink pig. 10 It is a big
happy pig. 11 It is a small white rabbit.

UNIT 05 ★
CULTURE

STORY 01 PP.18~19

1 beak   2 sour   3 first   4 second   5 third
6 ⓑ My mother calls me a prince.   7 ⓒ My
friends call me monkey.   8 ⓐ People call
me Jim.   9 We call David a hero.   10 People
call the bird a kiwi.   11 People call the
sour fruit a lemon.

STORY 02 PP.20~21

1 hold   2 tradition   3 tooth   4 invite
5 dessert   6 coin   7 What a lucky boy!
8 What an interesting tradition!   9 What
an exciting trip!   10 What a pretty doll!
11 What an interesting book!   12 What
cute puppies!

UNIT 06 ★
GOOD LUCK & BAD LUCK

STORY 01 PP.22~23

1 symbol   2 wave   3 bill   4 wallet
5 around the world   6 ⓑ Jinho is at the
theater.   7 ⓐ Mina is from Korea.
8 John is from the US.   9 He put the cat
doll at the front door.   10 He can't bring
an elephant from Thailand.

STORY 02 PP.24~25

1 fence   2 broken   3 sign   4 fail one's
test   5 mirror   6 ⓒ The clock is on the
wall.   7 ⓑ The bird is on the fence.
8 ⓐ The mirror is in the box.   9 A key is
on the chair.   10 A wallet is under the
chair.   11 The clock was on the table.

UNIT 07 ★
TRAVEL THE WORLD

STORY 01 PP.26~27

1 flush the toilet   2 careful   3 subway
4 rule   5 travel   6 pay a fine   7 ⓑ You
should not waste water.   8 ⓐ You should
be quiet in the classroom.   9 ⓒ You
should not eat anything in the library.
10 You should be careful.   11 You should
not feed birds.   12 You should not smoke.

STORY 02 PP.28~29

1 fun   2 worry   3 sleeping bag
4 afternoon   5 be made of   6 ⓐ Let's go
shopping.   7 ⓒ They want to go hiking.
8 ⓑ They will go swimming.   9 She will
go skiing.   10 He will go camping.
11 They will go ice fishing.

UNIT 08 ★
HOW STRANGE!

STORY 01 PP.30~31

1 terrible   2 try one's best   3 wear
4 step   5 win   6 playground   7 He
didn't wash his feet.   8 Ellis didn't win
the contest last week.   9 You didn't step
on my foot yesterday.   10 He didn't
wear socks.   11 Tim's friends didn't play
with him.   12 They didn't like his smelly
shoes.

STORY 02 PP.32~33

1 cover   2 stick   3 colorful   4 behavior
5 start   6 How long is the bridge?
7 How high is this tree?   8 How many
books are in your bag?   9 How high
is the train?   10 How many apples are
there?   11 How long is the ruler?

엄마의 부담은 덜고, 아이의 실력은 높이는 우리집 영어 시간!

초등영어
홈스쿨링이
된다!

초1~6

초3~6

초3~6

예비초~초2

★ **초등영어 리딩이 된다**
파닉스 마스터부터
교과 연계 리딩까지

★ **초등영어 단어가 된다**
교육부 권장 초등 필수
영단어 완전 분석

★ **초등영어 문법이 된다**
영문법 입문자를 위한
쉬운 개념 설명

★ **초등영어 파닉스가 된다**
철자 블랜딩(소리 조합) 연습으로
진짜 읽고 쓰기까지 가능

초등영어 된다 시리즈로 홈스쿨링 걱정 끝!

온라인 레벨테스트로
자녀 학습 수준에
딱 맞는 정확한 단계 선택

문법해설, 영상, 음원이
모두 들어있는
모바일 티칭 가이드

워크시트 등
다양한 무료 부가자료
서비스 제공

NE

www.nebooks.co.kr

발음 기호를 배워 봅시다.

하나의 알파벳이 여러 소리를 가지고 있는 경우가 있어서 같은 알파벳이라도 단어에 따라 소리가 달라집니다. 하지만 발음 기호를 알아두면 영어 단어를 정확하게 읽을 수 있답니다. 듣고 따라 하면서 발음 기호를 익혀봅시다.

★ 자음 ★

p	**plate** [pleit]		f	**feed** [fi:d]
b	**bad** [bæd]		v	**visit** [vízit]
t	**toy** [tɔi]		θ	**thing** [θiŋ]
d	**did** [did]		ð	**they** [ðei]
k	**cozy** [kóuzi]		s	**see** [si:]
g	**get** [get]		z	**zoo** [zu:]
tʃ	**chew** [tʃu:]		ʃ	**ship** [ʃip]
dʒ	**job** [dʒab]		ʒ	**vision** [víʒən]

h	**have** [həv]
m	**miss** [mis]
n	**note** [nout]
ŋ	**sing** [siŋ]

l	**leg** [leg]
r	**run** [rʌn]
j	**yes** [jes]
w	**weak** [wiːk]

☆ 모음 ☆

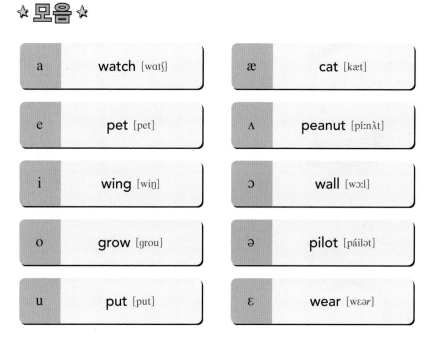

a	**watch** [wɑtʃ]
e	**pet** [pet]
i	**wing** [wiŋ]
o	**grow** [grou]
u	**put** [put]

æ	**cat** [kæt]
ʌ	**peanut** [píːnʌt]
ɔ	**wall** [wɔːl]
ə	**pilot** [páilət]
ɛ	**wear** [wɛər]

듣고 따라 말해 봅시다.

follow [fálou] 따라 하다

recipe [résəpì:] 조리법

knife [naif] 칼

cucumber [kjú:kʌmbər] 오이

carrot [kǽrət] 당근

4

add [æd] 더하다

dressing [drésiŋ] 드레싱, 소스

astronaut [ǽstrənɔ̀:t] 우주비행사

similar [símələr] 비슷한, 유사한

vegetable [védʒitəbl] 채소

 **dry** [drai] 마른, 건조한

 **hard** [hɑːrd] 딱딱한

 package [pǽkiʤ] **(포장용) 봉지**

 **pour** [pɔːr] 붓다

 microwave [máikrəwèiv]
전자레인지

the United States 미국

people [píːpl] 사람들

celebrate [séləbrèit] 기념하다

chocolate [tʃɔ́ːkəlit] 초콜렛

interesting [íntərəstiŋ]
흥미로운, 재미있는

each other 서로

pick up 집어 들다

future [fjúːtʃər] 미래

several [sévərəl] 몇몇의

choose [tʃuːz] 고르다

ball [bɔ:l] 공

 **money** [mʌ́ni] 돈

 athlete [ǽθliːt] 운동 선수

 **rich** [ritʃ] 부유한

듣고 따라 말해 봅시다.

prison [prízən] 감옥

peace [piːs] 평화

delivery [dilívəri] 배달

fast [fæst] 빠른

climb [klaim] 오르다

 **building** [bíldiŋ] 건물

 **drive** [draiv] 운전하다

 **cape** [keip] 망토

 **resemble** [rizémbl] 닮다

 **bat** [bæt] 박쥐

attack [ətǽk] 공격하다

young [jʌŋ] 어린

be afraid of 두려워하다

strong [strɔːŋ] 강한

train [trein] 단련하다

UNIT 04　MY PET

family [fǽməli] 가족

difficult [dífikʌ̀lt] 어려운

apartment [əpáːrtmənt] 아파트

bark [baːrk] 짖다

loudly [láudli] 큰 소리로

 **neighbor** [néibər] 이웃(사람)

 **angry** [ǽŋgri] 화가 난

 **allergic** [ələ́ːrdʒik] 알레르기가 있는

 **grow** [grou] 자라다

 **smart** [smɑːrt] 똑똑한

bathroom [bǽθrùːm]
욕실, 화장실

smile [smail] 웃다

greet [griːt] 반기다

guest [gest] 손님

clever [klévər] 영리한, 똑똑한

듣고 따라 말해 봅시다.

first [fəːrst] 첫 번째의

sour [sauər] (맛이) 신

second [sékənd] 두 번째의

beak [biːk] 부리

wing [wiŋ] 날개

fly [flai] 날다

third [θəːrd] 세 번째의

invite [inváit] 초대하다

dessert [dizə́ːrt] 디저트, 후식

tooth [tuːθ] 이
복수형 teeth

laugh [læf] 웃다

hold [hould] (손에) 들다, 잡다

과거형 held

coin [kɔin] 동전

congratulation
[kəngrætʃəléiʃən] 축하해요

tradition [trədíʃən] 전통

듣고 따라 말해 봅시다.

symbol [símbəl] 상징

around the world 전 세계

front door 현관, 정문

wave [weiv] 흔들다

bill [bil] 지폐

 **wallet** [wɑ́lit] 지갑

 **elephant** [éləfənt] 코끼리

 **bring** [briŋ] 가져오다

 **have a test** 시험이 있다

 clock [klɑk] 시계

mirror [mírər] 거울

broken [bróukən] 깨진

fence [fens] 울타리

sign [sain] 징조

fail one's test
시험을 못 보다, 낙제하다

travel [trǽvəl] 여행하다

careful [kέərfəl] 조심스러운

rule [ruːl] 규칙

subway [sʌ́bwèi] 지하철

feed [fiːd] 먹이를 주다

park [pɑ:rk] 공원

flush the toilet
변기의 물을 내리다

pay a fine 벌금을 내다

be made of ~로 만들어지다

worry [wə́:ri] 걱정하다

sleep [sliːp] 자다

warm [wɔːrm] 따뜻한, 따스한

sleeping bag [slíːpiŋ bǽg] 침낭

fun [fʌn] 재미

afternoon [æ̀ːftərnúːn] 오후

win [win] 우승하다

과거형 won

contest [kántest] 대회

try one's best 최선을 다하다

terrible [térəbl] 심한, 지독한

wear [wɛər] 입다

과거형 wore

sock [sɑk] 양말

playground [pléigràund]
운동장

step [step] 밟다

foot [fut] 발

복수형 feet

smelly [sméli] 냄새나는

stick [stik] 붙이다

behavior [bihéivjər] 행동

colorful [kʌ́lərfəl]
(색이) 다채로운, 알록달록한

cover [kʌ́vər] 덮다

start [stɑːrt] 시작되다